MW01096320

Finding Janine

By

Chiufang Hwang, M.D.

Finding Janine, Published December, 2017

Editorial and proofreading services: Kathleen A. Tracy, Karen Grennan

Interior layout and cover design: Howard Johnson

Photo credits:

Front cover image: "Abstract background of woman silhouette," designed by Freepik

All photographs are the sole owner of the author, Chiufang Hwang, M.D.

 **SDP Publishing**

Published by SDP Publishing, an imprint of SDP Publishing Solutions, LLC.

All rights reserved. No part of the material protected by this copyright notice may be reproduced or utilized in any form or by any means, electronic or mechanical, including photocopying, recording, or by any information storage and retrieval system, without written permission from the copyright owner.

To obtain permission(s) to use material from this work, please submit a written request to:

SDP Publishing
Permissions Department
PO Box 26, East Bridgewater, MA 02333
or email your request to info@SDPPublishing.com.

ISBN-13 (print): 978-0-9992839-2-9
e-ISBN-13 (ebook): 978-0-9992839-3-6

Library of Congress Control Number: 2017960251

Copyright 2017, Chiufang Hwang, MD

Printed in the United States of America

Dedication

To Janine, who at ten years old embraced me into her culture and help me find my American voice. Your influence has been indelible and still informs how I see the world and how I think of myself. The lingo, the food, and big Mama are forever reflected in my adult self.

Table of Contents

Introduction

The ironic thing about the past is that it is never really behind us because it's a constant part of us. Every encounter, every connection—eternally memorable or quickly forgotten—forever lives inside us because who we are today is the sum total of all those experiences. We're a complex tapestry, with each thread bearing a name or occasion from days gone by. Most people are aware of how their parents inform the adults they became. My second published book, *Grown-Up Child,* explored that family dynamic in great detail. Like many immigrant children from Asian countries, I assumed an adult role by default, growing up because of my parents' inability to—and disinterest in—assimilating into the American culture. I grew up far before my time, and I suffered the consequences.

But my personality, attitudes, and perspectives were also influenced by scores of others who provided me a window into their own families' ethnic cultures and traditions. At the time, I was merely trying to fit in. Born in Taiwan, my mother and I immigrated to the United States to join my father, who was on a quixotic quest for a PhD. I was two years old, so America is the only country I've ever known.

They say the United States is a melting pot; well, my family was more like a white rice cooker. Under my parents' roof it was Little Taiwan wherever we lived. And as a couple they only sought out other Taiwanese immigrants to socialize with. I suspect my mother found comfort in having a shared language since she never really learned English. But as we moved across the South—from Texas to South Carolina and back as my father pursued one graduate program after another—my classmates, my babysitters, and our neighbors exposed me to a very different world.

One that was racially, socially, and culturally diverse.

One that was loud, argumentative, and informal.

One where children spoke their minds and parents openly showed affection.

One that offered freedom as well as peril.

One that gave a shy, diminutive girl a sense of independence that would have been unheard of in her native land.

How those experiences informed who I am today have become much more apparent to me through the process of writing books. And it's made me reflect on the childhood friends who expanded my horizons and gave me the freedom to express who I really was. At home my parents expected me to play the role of the dutiful, obeisant daughter. I was expected to do and not say—anything. But with the children of my youth, I could be just another American kid.

That all of my school and project peers were either white or black was not an issue. I didn't grow up with issues about skin color or ethnicity. (If I had a bias it was against mean people. And that still holds true.) I was the token Asian and happy to hang with any kids willing to have me. And the one who embraced me more than anyone was Janine. Janine was my best friend in grade school when we lived in Columbia, South Carolina. She was my protector. And in many ways she was also my mentor, tutoring me on the ways of black culture—how to take an attitude, how to talk, how to dance, how to have swagger ... the latter not an easy thing when you're barely four feet tall.

Even though I only lived in Columbia a short time, it was a seminal time, and Janine was front and center. When my father announced we were moving yet again after another failed attempt to secure his doctorate, I cried knowing I would never have a friend quite like Janine ever again. And I didn't. But life goes on, and eventually the memories get shelved and gather dust and before you know it decades have passed.

Then I decided to write a book about the balancing act of growing up caught between cultures. While putting my first draft of *Grown-Up Child* together in 2014, I recounted some of my adventures with Janine and how our friendship impacted me, in ways I could only truly appreciate in retrospect.

The memories prompted me to try and reconnect with Janine. I did a Facebook search, but nothing popped. Then I tried LinkedIn. Nada. Instagram was also a bust. I assumed she had gotten married, changed her last name, and was now forever lost to me.

In 2016 I wrote another book, *American Sweetheart*, which was published later that year. As I was reading it through one last time before it went back to the publisher, I came to this passage about my last day with Janine:

> *I waited until we were sitting together on the bus on my last day before telling her (my family was leaving). We both cried and cried. We had never lived anywhere long enough for me to form close friendships, except for Janine. So leaving was hard on me. But it's always harder on the one left behind. She wailed, heartbroken and worried about who was going to protect me. We corresponded for months after I moved. In her long, long, handwritten letters,*

she told me how much she missed me. I dearly loved
my friend Janine.
We never saw each other again.

So once again, I set out to find Janine. The childhood friend who represented my transition from a first-generation immigrant to American youth. The uninhibited girl who taught me to laugh at myself. The protector who was my partner in crime as I learned a certain amount of subversiveness was necessary if I was ever going to become my own woman and get out from under the shadow of my Old World parents.

Social media was still useless, but this time when I Googled her name, I got a hit. Not for Janine but for her sister's obituary, which listed the surviving family. That's how I found out Janine's married name. And I was eventually able to track her down.

Finding Janine is both about reconnecting with my old childhood friend and the very different paths our lives took—I ended up a psychiatrist, she still lives in Columbia near her childhood home. But it's also about how I found myself and how our friendship helped me give my inner American a voice while still respecting my heritage. All kids have to make the same journey, but for immigrant children and teens, the road comes with a few extra challenges. But the diverse communities where my family lived helped me feel like less an outsider and also showed me there was a big world out there beyond my parents' chosen culturally insular life. Our family and ethnicity influence us, but we are not defined by either. That's the true power of a melting pot—you can take the best of all cultures and make it your own.

One Monday in January 2017, several months after I found Janine, I was in Los Angeles for a conference. She called me at 2:30 p.m. on a Sunday afternoon to tell me about a dream she'd had. In it, people were picking on me. And she got so upset that anyone would mess with me that it woke her up. The dream was so vivid that it felt like a premonition. Other than LA traffic about to be the death of me, I assured her I was fine.

We talked for a long time, and I told her about the clinic that my husband—who I call Doc—and I have run since 2003. In the waiting room I have several paintings of an old Southern hog slaughterhouse. It's not at all graphic, just artistic. There's a print of a low country recipe for shrimp and grits. And we have a collection of art books featuring different African-American artists—all things that remind me of my upbringing.

I told her that recently one of my husband's patients asked him, "Doctor, may I ask you … is your wife a black artist?"

That is not the first time he'd been asked. Doc usually responds, "No, but she grew up in the culture."

Well, this time he joked, "Everything about her is, except her skin color."

Janine laughed. "That's true; damn right you're one of us."

I told her, "You know, in Asian culture, when they think you've become too Americanized and not deferential enough to our family culture, they'll call you a banana—white inside and yellow on the outside. So what would they call me?"

Janine thought a moment. "Well, you ain't white, and you ain't Chinese. Everything about you is black except your skin color. So you're a little bit brownish inside, a little rough on the edges, and yellow on the outside. Girl, you're a plantain."

So whatever fruit or vegetable or spice you may be in our country's melting pot stew, this book was written to celebrate that diversity and to offer a first-hand perspective of the immigrant experience.

Chapter 1

發現

*A*ppearances can be deceiving. My résumé screams accomplishment: psychiatrist, mother of two college students, successful marriage, member of several associations. I'm professional in manner and appearance.

And then I open my mouth.

Because I'm Taiwanese-American, some people assume I might have an accent. And I do. But not the *Flower Drum Song* one they expect. I sound like grits and chitlins come to life. And not the smooth drawl of my fellow Texans, but the rough-edged, down-home dialect of the inner-city South with the added spice of African-American intonation and attitude. You can take the girl out of the Columbia, South Carolina, projects but her accent will always belie her upbringing.

And did I mention attitude? When you grow up on the streets, an in-your-face response is always simmering just below the surface, even with the stateliest of demeanors. The moment someone angers me or tries to shortchange me in some way or threatens me, the decorum I've spent my entire adult life cultivating goes right out the window, and I revert to the tough-talking, proceed-at-your-peril, girl of my youth. If I bristle at the clinic, one of my longtime coworkers will say: *Ah, Dr. Hwang's street side's coming out.* It's kind of an office joke. If I do it in public, people are taken aback. But they also stop messing with me. Considering I'm barely five feet tall, that's a result I can live with, unseemly be damned.

I acquired my incongruous Southern accent from the black kids who were my companions. That's just one of many ways my ethnically and culturally diverse upbringing informs who I am today. I have definitely achieved the immigrant-child-makes-good American dream, but it was a gritty road from South Carolina to med school. While such a story is hardly new, my experiences were unique in that I spent my childhood and teen years as a minority among minorities. No matter where we lived—from Texas to South Carolina to Alabama—I was the token Chinese girl in the neighborhood and in school. At that time there weren't many Asians in the Deep South. Or at least not in the places where we lived. Blacks and whites alike considered us exotic. A novelty. And on at least one occasion, newsworthy. In second grade I made the front page of the *Columbia Record* because I was one of only two Asians who had started school that year. Our fathers were both graduate students.

And that's what had brought my mother and me to the United States. My father was pursuing a doctorate, and we joined him when I was two. I came across our passport picture recently, and I was struck by how young and happy my mother looks. It's clear she's full of anticipation for the adventure ahead. I'm two, but even then I look worried. Apparently I was born expecting the worst when it came to my parents.

Our first home was in Hempstead, Texas, where we lived for about a year because my father had a teaching job there.

We lived on a farm, and all I remember are a lot of chickens. No people, just poultry. Then we went to Rock Hill, South Carolina, which was just a half hour outside of Charlotte, North Carolina, for my father's next job. My earliest memory there was noticing that everyone—the dean, the students, the administrators—was black, except us.

We lived on campus in a trailer located right behind the dean's office. Our housing was free in exchange for my mother doing some clerical tasks for the math department. Even though she knew no English, she was very good at understanding how to do tasks between hand gestures, pointing, and showing.

We shared our trailer with an Indian man who was a graduate student. The trailer had two bedrooms, one on either side, with a kitchen and the living room in the middle. In the beginning, every time I saw our trailer-mate I'd ask: *Who* IS *that man?* But my mother would just shush me. I finally asked my father, who said the man was also teaching at the school and that's why he was with us. He was quiet, had no wife or children, and kept to himself. After a while I hardly noticed him anymore.

In the evenings we'd go out and walk around the campus, and eventually I learned that Friendship College was somewhat famous. It was founded in 1891 and began with eleven students. It eventually was chartered as a black junior college in the early 1900s, making it one of the oldest black colleges. In 1961, several years before we arrived, a group of Friendship College students staged a sit-in at a segregated lunch counter in Rock Hill. After they had been arrested, the students refused bail. It became a Civil Rights strategy called *jail, no bail,* which prevented municipalities from earning money by arresting protesters. The students became known as the Friendship Nine and made the college a symbol of the Civil Rights movement. By the time we arrived, the protests were long over, but the events remained campus lore. And it was my first exposure to what African-Americans had been willing to sacrifice for equal rights.

Although it was a quiet town, Rock Hill's surrounding region had an interesting past. For generations going back to colonial days, the area around the town was mostly agricultural with peach orchards and strawberry and vegetable fields. There are two nearby rivers, the Broad and the Catawba River, and a lot of parks and greenery. The area is the home of the Catawba Indian Nation, who are now known for their skill as pottery artisans. But back before Europeans settled the region, the tribe lived off the land hunting, farming, fishing, and trading with settlers. Settlers eventually established cotton plantations.

During the Revolutionary War colonists fought several battles against the British in the area, including the Battle of Huck's Defeat in July 1780, which was a significant British defeat. After the war the area prospered. In the 1840s the Charlotte and South Carolina Railroad Company proposed building a railroad from Charlotte to Columbia, SC. Locals worried about the potential noise and pollution prompted the railroads to locate the track near a rocky spot that had long been a familiar landmark for travelers. The surveyors designated the area *rocky hill*. The original post office was opened in April 1852 and called Ebenezer Depot. It was quickly settled by merchants, banks, and utilities and thrived. Instead of shipping the locally-grown cotton to New England for processing, speculators built mills, along with a buggy and carriage maker, machine shops, iron works, and a furniture-maker. In 1896 the name was changed to Rockhill, which became Rock Hill sixteen years later. The town was dotted with churches of varying denominations, segregated into black and white well past the legal end of segregation with the passage of the Civil Rights Act of 1964.

The most fun fact about our new home was York, a town about ten miles away, had been the winter home for the Bennett Brothers Circus (later called the Wallace Brothers Circus) from the late 1920s through the 1940s. A family-run show, the circus featured performers and a few animals. During the winter hiatus the troupe designed and trained for new shows and enjoyed some R&R. That was something that my father would have liked to see. He enjoyed going to places off the beaten path to see unusual attractions.

But at that time he was consumed with his job. And with both my parents working—my father teaching and my mother doing the clerical work in the math department—I was put in daycare. The daycare center wasn't on the campus or affiliated with Friendship College. It was located somewhere in the lower town. I wasn't old enough yet for regular school, so my parents parked me there. I felt abandoned. Every morning after my father dropped me off, I'd go inside then run to the window and wave at him as he drove away. I was so sad he was leaving me. But after I got used to the new surroundings, I stopped running to the window. I still felt abandoned.

Daycare was where I started learning English although I hardly ever spoke it around my parents. It was all Taiwanese all the time in our trailer. At daycare I was very shy and barely said anything to anyone there either. I'd just hang around other kids silently. Even after I was perfectly bilingual, I chose not to talk. Everyone probably thought I was mute. My silence was obviously a defense mechanism. I was still adjusting to being in a new country where we didn't know anyone.

Even though my mother didn't speak English, my father did. He had scored well on the TOEFL—test of English as a foreign language—and the Graduate Record Examination, a standardized test that is an admissions requirement for most graduate schools in the United States. He had to score high on both to get in the United States on a student visa. Actually, from hearing him talk to others, his grammar was much better than mine, which got worse and worse over the years because of the kids I hung around. But we never spoke English to one another, so I was always very conscious of going from one culture to another every time I came home to the trailer from school. As I got older sometimes it felt like I didn't fully belong in either.

I certainly didn't relate to my Taiwanese heritage, even if I dressed the part. My maternal grandmother regularly sent me clothes. Considering my size, I literally looked like a little China doll wearing the outfits she sent. But Taiwan was a place I didn't know, nor could I appreciate it at that age. So my parent's insistence on clinging to the customs and language of what to me was a foreign place made it harder for me to feel completely settled in my new country.

When I wasn't working on math problems my father gave me, he would occasionally take me for a walk in the evenings. Sometimes we went to the cafeteria, but mostly we'd wander around the campus. One night we were returning to the trailer. It was still really hot out, and I was in no hurry to go back inside. Turned out to be one of my first be-careful-what-you-wish-for lessons. Blocking our way in was a snake. We stood there frozen, not knowing what to do. (The snake too.)

A black man happened to walk by. He was athlete big and was one of my father's students. My father asked him for help. The young man looked down at the snake.

"Don't worry about it; let me get something. Just stay away from it."

He came back in a few minutes carrying a small lamp, a stick, and a jar. He shone the light on the snake and moved it into the jar. I thought it was very cool.

It wasn't the first time one of my father's students would

come to the rescue. The trailer we lived in was small, and the bathroom was cramped. One day I used the bathroom, and when I went to leave, the door had locked. I had no idea how to unlock it. I was stuck. There was a small, vent window in the bathroom, but it was too high for me to reach. I called for my parents and kept saying: *I can't get out. I can't get out.*

My dad was trying the handle and yelling: *Unlock the door. Unlock the door.*

I'm sure half the campus heard us. A couple of students came to our trailer to see what was wrong. The tallest of them got on one of his friend's shoulders, pulled out the vent window, reached his arm down into the bathroom, and pulled me out. Had I been an average-sized kid, I would have never fit. Being a micro-human saved me that day. I have no memory of how they finally got the bathroom door open—I assume they removed the door knob—but after that I wouldn't close doors anymore, and to this day I'm afraid of getting locked in a room.

I now wonder if those two incidents predisposed me to feel safe and protected around African-Americans because it would be a recurring theme in my life growing up.

When school let out for the summer in Rock Hill, my daycare ballooned with older kids, like from third to sixth grade. They'd occasionally load us up in the van for a field trip. All the older kids would want me to sit in the middle or would cradle me. They were always very possessive of me and wanted to be around me because I was so tiny and Chinese. These were all white kids, and I was just as much of a novelty to them.

I think what I remember most about the people I met in Rock Hill during our year there was that everyone seemed to have a purpose. Even from the windows of our trailer, you could sense the energy from being on a college campus. My father's students were well-spoken, ambitious, confident, and very polite. They all had an eye toward the future and often talked about their goals and the kinds of work they wanted to do or the degrees they were pursuing. I'd even gotten used to our trailer-mate.

I found the people and the environment exciting and comforting; hopefulness and anticipation of good things to come were in the air. Dreams seemed in reach, even for my dad. But I'd learn soon enough that life wasn't always equitable and the world could be a very scary place, especially for those who didn't quite fit in

Chapter 2

發現

I'm not exactly a glass half full kind of person. It's not that I'm a pessimist exactly. I prefer to think of it as being prepared. I learned at a young age that calamity happens. My most vivid memory of Rock Hill is watching our trailer burn. As in firemen, red emergency lights flashing, and scorched earth. To my three-year-old eyes, it seemed much more dramatic than it was. The fire started in the half occupied by our roommate, so his room was charbroiled. Our side smelled like a barbecue but was intact. The fire started at noon when none of us were home, so nobody was injured.

The firemen told us the propane tank had blown up. It was the middle of summer, very hot and humid, reaching at least ninety degrees on most days. I remember the gravel being so hot that it burned my feet through my cheap flip-flops. In retrospect, I'm surprised exploding propane tanks weren't a regular occurrence.

I don't recall ever seeing our trailer-mate again. But we continued staying in the trailer after the fire. It was free housing, and my parents weren't picky. What was a little soot? The next school year in 1970, the University of South Carolina (USC) accepted my father into its PhD mathematics program, so we moved to Columbia, which was seventy miles south of Rock Hill. Our zip code might have changed, but our living conditions didn't. Our new home was in a low-income housing project that looked like a run-down Army barracks. There were 110 two-bedroom apartments in Henley Homes, and all qualified residents were assigned units with free electricity and very low rent. Mercifully, there wasn't a propane tank in sight.

That summer I attended the Henley Homes Day Care and Kindergarten, which was right inside the project. There were no ESL programs for children there—we were lucky to have tables and chairs—so I continued acquiring English in a hit-and-miss sort of way. The handful of other Chinese kids in the school spoke different dialects, so the only language we had in common was our rudimentary English. No surprise, then, that my kindergarten experience didn't remotely prepare me for first grade at the St. Andrews branch of Timmerman, the private school I attended.

My father found out about the school through a Taiwanese professor at USC, who was sending his five-year-old there. It was a new grade one through six elementary school—so new that there was still construction going on when I showed up for my first day—and the administration was actively looking for students to fill the seats. The kids had to test into it, but those who passed got to attend for free. And they were accepting kids as young as five.

When my father caught wind of that, he had me take the test. I passed, and he signed me up. He liked the idea of me starting school at five. Not because I was so smart; I wasn't. I was good at math but everybody else there was already reading fluently, while I couldn't even manage *The*

Very Hungry Caterpillar. But it didn't matter that I was way behind in my language skills. Many immigrant Chinese families enrolled their children in school as early as possible, and my father joined that trend. But the school was quite a drive, so my father and some other graduate students took turns carpooling.

Despite my age, I didn't feel younger than the others; just exponentially shorter. Although I was struggling with reading, I felt that I was in the right grade. I suspect that was my defense mechanism, an immigrant version of *Love the One You're With.* On one hand I was always going to be the different one on so many levels that age was the least of my concerns. So I made myself at home as best I could in whatever situation I found myself.

I can now see that I took the opposite tack my parents did. For a long time when I thought about my parents, it would be familiar images from childhood. I'd recall their constant bickering, my mother's passive aggressiveness, my father's preoccupation with pursuing his academic Holy Grail, my mother's cooking, and her willingness to have me be the English-speaking family front man even at a young age.

But those are the imprinted images of a child. They take emotional root and tend to obscure a more objective perspective. It wasn't until I was married with practically grown children, that I ever considered my parents through adult eyes, minus the dysfunctional family baggage.

My father left Taiwan five months after I was born in March of 1966. He had gotten accepted at Mississippi State University, so he left my mother and me behind, came to the United States and spent two and a half years earning his master's degree in mathematics—even though he had already earned the equivalent of a bachelor's and master's in math in Taiwan. But before he could pursue a PhD in the United

States, he had to earn a master's at an American college. At least, that's how it was later explained to me.

At that time the graduate programs were filled with international students competing against each other for the few openings for PhD programs. With my father, we met several Kenyan and Nigerian graduate students on our walks around campus. They were older than most—in their late twenties—and very focused on their goals. Most of them had families to support. I marveled at how dark they were, compared to the African-Americans in my school and our neighborhood. They had already received their bachelor's degrees in Africa, but again, it didn't matter what degrees you got from your own country. You had to start fresh. So my family did.

Once my father earned his master's in Mississippi, my mother and I were allowed to come to the United States. Since my father immigrated to America pursuing a dream, he had more incentive to assimilate than my mother did, who only immigrated here to follow my father. Given her druthers, she would have stayed in Taiwan with her family and comfortable lifestyle.

I think in general my father was more outgoing, one reason he chose teaching. He enjoyed the interaction with his peers and students. He sought out conversations and had a genuine interest in their interests. The Russell House University Union had a recreation area, and we would meander through there, stopping to meet people and talk.

One day, as we took a shortcut through a coed dorm, we heard someone playing a baby grand piano in the lobby. The music was wonderful. We made our way to the piano and the skinny, young black man playing. He was wearing sunglasses and was playing without sheet music. At the end of the next song my father complimented him and asked what songs he'd been playing.

The pianist smiled. "Some Scott Joplin. 'Maple Leaf Rag'

and before that 'The Entertainer.'" As he spoke I realized the man was blind.

We stayed and listened to him play several more songs. In between my dad asked how he had learned to play so well, what he was studying on campus, and how he managed to keep up with his studies. A very good thing about my dad was how well he drew out people he'd never met before. People loved to tell him their stories. I really liked that about my father, and I enjoyed those times immensely.

My mother was social in her own way. Where my father was comfortable stopping and talking to complete strangers, my mother's social circle was smaller. She made a friend or two at work—usually another Taiwanese immigrant—who she would go visit over a cup of tea. Her friends—one was a professor's wife—grew Chinese vegetables in their garden so my mother would pick up a *loofa*, a kind of Chinese gourd. Back then in Columbia there were no Whole Foods, and no Asian vegetables were sold at the supermarkets either. So these private gardens gave the local Taiwanese immigrants a comforting taste of home.

When we were in Rock Hill, there wasn't much socializing. We were stuck on campus, and it was a very insular kind of existence. But once we got to Columbia my parents' social life picked up, even if it didn't exactly broaden. Somehow my dad became acquainted with a man named Dr. Ling. He had earned his PhD in mathematics at Notre Dame and was in his first year of teaching math at South Carolina State College, which is in Orangeburg. The school is South Carolina's only public, historically black college and university and has been around since the nineteenth century.

Once a month on a Friday night we would make the hour drive to Orangeburg so my dad could visit with Dr. Ling. We'd arrive around seven or eight o'clock, and Dr. Ling would help my dad with his math by checking his work. They would huddle together for hours in the kitchen, often until midnight, as math gave way to a discussion about the world in general and Taiwan in particular.

My mother and Mrs. Ling would sit together, chatting about whatever to pass the time, and I would hang out with their daughter. Her name was Jean, and she was a couple of years younger than me although we were the same size. We'd go into her room and play with her toys and dolls—a nice break from having to do math problems. I enjoyed going over there because she had a lot of toys. They also lived in a row of faculty housing but had much nicer things because Dr. Ling was a full professor. They had a piano, and Jean had a little table with a little phone. And they had Jell-O, which seemed like an exotic treat to me.

For as long as we lived in Columbia, we'd go visit the Lings one Friday every month. Sometimes my mother would bring some dried noodles, and Mrs. Ling would cook them so we could have dinner together. But except for the visits, my parents had no contact with the Lings. We didn't have a phone at the time because it was expensive to have a phone line. Or at least, expensive for us.

But I think their bond went beyond helping my dad with his math proofs; they were bound by Taiwanese politics. Dr. Ling was very anti-Chiang Kai-shek, as was my father. The very short version is the Chinese Nationalist Party—called the Kuomintang—was the dominant political party of China from 1928 to 1949 and was led by Chiang. Those who supported the Kuomintang called themselves Nationalists. Chiang's opposition to communism led to harsh policies. People suspected of communist sympathies were tortured and executed in public, in an attempt to terrify political opponents into submission. It didn't work.

In 1949, Chiang Kai-shek lost to the Communists led by Mao Tse-tung. Chiang and two million of his Nationalist followers fled to Taiwan, where he established the Republic of China and assumed leadership of the island. On February 28 of that year, Chiang had tens of thousands of Taiwanese citizens executed, including scholars, intellectuals, and community leaders—anyone who resisted him. Known as the Kuomintang's White Terror, the goal was to quash any political dissidents.

Chiang remained the island's military dictator for almost thirty years and ruled under martial law, which most native Taiwanese hated. So that's how Mr. Ling and my father bonded. They would commiserate about how bad the government was under Chiang, and they were both convinced if they tried going back to Taiwan, the government would cripple them. Not exactly the fun, happy conversations for a kid to hear.

Many Taiwanese immigrants of the late 1960s and early 1970s came to the United States to get away from what they felt were Chiang's repressive policies. Mr. Ling sought out any and all Taiwanese immigrants he could find; I suppose looking to create a community. His version of a Taiwan-town. I presume that's how he and my father originally connected. Through Dr. Ling's connections, we met another family, the Chans. Dr. Chan also worked at South Carolina State College, teaching English, ironically enough.

One Christmas, Dr. Ling also introduced us to a Taiwanese family who lived in Greenville, which was more than one hundred miles away. So we piled in the car and went to visit, probably unannounced. There were about four families in all my parents would visit. And they always seemed happy for the company, even when it wasn't expected. Unlike American couples, in Taiwanese culture rarely did a husband

and wife go out for date night alone. My parents never did any such thing nor did the other couples they knew. So those visits were the main social thing we did. But for all the road trips we took, I don't recall any of them coming to visit us. I think part of that was my dad genuinely liked going on road trips; it was a way of getting out of our cramped apartment.

My father was much different by himself than he was with other people. My father was and still is very easy to get along with when talking about academics or sharing small talk with students or peers. He seemed to have an insatiable curiosity about other people. That's where I learned my talking skills. Anytime he ever had to wait in line he'd end up starting a conversation with the person next to him. The few times we had visitors, he would be the chatty, congenial host. But once company was gone, he tended to be lost in his own world. It wasn't that he was absent-minded as much as he was so focused on his endless PhD goal everything fell by the wayside. Like his wife and kids.

You know how people tend to have a public face and a private face? My mother was pretty much the same regardless of her environment. She wasn't particularly communicative in any language. I suspect that was one reason my father sought out conversations with strangers so much. If it were left to her, I doubt we would have ever gone to visit anyone. She went because she was supposed to as a dutiful wife. But I think it was good we went because it gave my mother a chance to be around people who spoke the same language and had grown up in the same place.

I suppose it says something that Jean and I only spoke English to each other. While our parents found comfort, or at least familiarity, in their native tongue and shared political views, their spawn was much more interested in fitting in with the kids at school and in our neighborhoods. Looking back, that might not have been the best idea, considering where my family lived.

Our housing project was full of surprises, not always the good kind. One chilly night in December when I was five years old, I woke up in a panic around 2:00 a.m. to the sharp, piercing noise of shattered glass hitting the asphalt in our parking lot. Turned out someone was doing a bit of early Christmas shopping, and the gift was going to be our ailing 1968 Plymouth. With a BB gun in hand, the perpetrator shot out the glass of the driver's side window so he could unlock the door, jump in, and speed off. But the best-laid plans of mice and men and car thieves ...

My father's faded clunker had carburetor problems and wouldn't cooperate with the car thief's fast and furious dreams of a speedy getaway. Half the time, he couldn't get it to start either. After the would-be thief tried and failed to get the engine to turn over, he gave up.

"Guy damn muthafocka!" he cursed in disgust as he slammed the door then ran off.

I didn't feel particularly violated or offended that someone would try to steal from us. I figured they simply needed a car so why not steal from the newbies on the block. But I was annoyed that the thief broke the window because it meant freezing on my way to school until my father could afford to have the pane replaced.

Several months later when the weather was warmer and the days longer, we were eating dinner. I never saw my mother sit down to eat, and I usually ate while walking around. My father was sitting at a table provided by a local church that accepted donations from people who wanted to get rid of old furniture. It was still daylight, the sun not yet setting.

It was a Saturday. The complex had washing machines but no dryers. So my mother had hung the laundry out to dry on the clothesline right outside our back door. Through the screen door, we could see my father's new Fruit of the Loom underwear all lined up in a neat row, gently flapping in the breeze. He had splurged on some undershirts and boxer shorts at Kmart after his ratty, old ones finally fell apart. On either side of the underwear, birds were perched on the clothesline chattering or taking a moment to groom.

Just as my mother was setting a bowl of rice on the table, the birds flew off in a collective flurry of alarmed chirps and beating wings. By the time we looked out the screen door to see what had startled the birds, someone had stolen all of my father's shiny new underwear and were already long gone. My father jumped up, but then abruptly slumped back down. Really, what would he do if he actually caught the thief? My father wasn't a physically imposing man. Although the odds were it was just some kid, better to go without underwear than take the chance it was someone older who might be carrying a weapon. It should be noted that nobody was ever interested in stealing my clothes. They probably thought they were dolls' clothes.

Henley Homes apparently wasn't that safe a place day or night, but I would go outside to play anyway. Shortly after the underwear theft, I was playing with some other welfare kids who lived there. I wasn't very good at sports or outdoor children's games; I couldn't even climb the monkey bars because I wasn't very nimble or flexible. My parents stressed academics and very much discouraged sports or outdoor activities. I looked frail because of my size and both my parents wanted me to be feminine and not get my knees skinned.

On one hand, at that age I was the most stereotypical little Chinese immigrant you could find: quiet, unquestioning, and apparently obedient. I would never overtly challenge my parents. But I didn't always follow their wishes when they weren't around. While they might have wanted a China doll, I had the heart of a tomboy. I'd run around with the other kids. I was once outside playing when a shard of glass pierced my cheap flip-flops and gashed my foot. My mother had to clean and wrap the wound, but I was right back outside the next day.

Like a lot of kids, my circle of acquaintances at home were different from school friends that first year because nobody else in our projects was going to private school. But once Timmerman got its enrollment up, they expected tuition, so the next school year, I would have my first taste of the Columbia public school system.

Chapter 3

發現

The culture shock of going from the suburban Timmerman to an inner-city school was jarring even for me who was born able to go with the flow.

Timmerman was primarily white. In fact, I'd never seen so many white kids under one roof before in my life. My father had tended to work at traditionally black colleges in the South, and we had often lived in the rural South, so I was used to more diversity. But even compared to the white kids I knew in the projects, the suburban students at Timmerman seemed like a different species, they were so well-dressed and well-mannered.

But once again, I didn't feel out of place. For one thing, I didn't call attention to myself, the teachers liked me because I was quiet and attentive, and I was non-threatening, so I avoided any mean girl antics. I also didn't look out of place, thanks to my maternal grandmother, who was still regularly sending me new clothes from Taiwan. Had I been white or black, wearing silk tunics and kimono-type tops may have looked like I was dressing up in a cross-cultural Halloween costume. But on me it simply looked natural and an homage to my heritage. I am Taiwanese woman/child, hear me roar.

I apparently earned style points with the Timmerman faculty. One time the two teachers on recess duty called me over to join them. I looked around to make sure they were motioning to me. I knew I hadn't done anything wrong, so I was curious why I was suddenly singled out. But even then, I loved attention, so I happily walked over, eager to please.

They admired the dress I was wearing, which was a dress that my mother had altered to look like a tunic. One of the teachers turned me around and held the hem out to see the intricate workmanship and feel the silky fabric. They *oohed* and *aahed* over the detail and asked if my mother had made it for me. She hadn't, but she always had to alter the clothes my grandmother sent because they were usually too big for me. My mother was a decent seamstress, so I always looked good.

For as much as the teachers were charmed, my classmates didn't seem to care; they probably expected their peers to be well-dressed. I didn't do too much during recess. I was mindful of taking care of my good clothes; my parents certainly couldn't afford to replace them. Plus, truth be told, I liked looking stylish. And yes, I readily admit I haven't changed much in that regard.

The only time I felt painfully out of step and out of place was during lunch. The school didn't have a cafeteria, and even if it had, my parents wouldn't have given me money to buy lunch. After recess we'd come in, and everyone would eagerly open their lunch boxes or brown bags. I watched with envy as kids pulled out celery sticks and bologna sandwiches—which to me seemed so exotic. Every day was a new misery. One day it was a boiled egg. Another it was some type of boiled vegetable. It wasn't Taiwanese. It wasn't Chinese. And it wasn't anything known to the average American. It was whatever she found in the refrigerator and put in the pot.

If it happened to be hot, whatever concoction she had made would ferment so when I opened my container, a pungent aroma would waft through the room, prompting a chorus of *Gross. That smells. What is that you're eating?* I felt like asking them: *How do you think I feel? I'm supposed to eat this.* It isn't that Taiwanese food is inherently unappetizing. Quite the contrary. Dishes like beef noodle soup, minced pork belly on rice, and scallion pancakes are popular with a lot of people. On the other hand, there are some dishes that definitely fall under the acquired taste label. The problem was my mother was a disinterested cook. And a lazy cook. Which equaled a lousy cook.

A typical meal consisted of white rice with beef chunks and green beans. The greasy gravy came from cooking the meat, and my mother poured it over the rice. She also cooked pinkish fried rice, made of frozen mixed vegetables, cooked rice, and ketchup. Sometimes we had cabbage or Chinese cabbage, but there wasn't much flavor to those, so she'd add a ton of MSG, which was a popular condiment before all its health risks were detailed. My mother would buy containers of it at the local Piggly Wiggly.

Rather than adopt American lunches—I would have traded my favorite silk kimono for a peanut butter and jelly sandwich—she stubbornly clung to her Taiwanese roots. The more she refused to assimilate, the more I wanted to embrace my adopted culture. Or I should say cultures plural because saying America is a melting pot isn't just a cliché; it's an apt description.

After I finished first grade, my parents had to figure out what to do with me. My mother was working at a factory, and my father was attending his classes at the University of South

Carolina. Their solution was to put my father in charge of me for the summer. What could possibly go wrong?

For the most part, I spent that summer sequestered in the campus library. My father would drop me off in the morning before his first class with a warning to stay put. He would come get me at noon and take me to lunch at a nearby USC eatery where he'd order me a hamburger. Whether his motive was pity or blackmail, I didn't care. Those hamburgers were the highlight of my summer.

A half hour later he stashed me back at the library, where I'd kill time until 5:00 or 6:00 in the evening. My father never asked me what I did all day. No one in the library ever asked why I was there alone all day. So I did what you usually do in a library; I read. My favorite book initially was the unabridged dictionary. But then I discovered the *Encyclopedia Britannica*, which became my best friend. I was not yet a good reader, but all of the articles were illustrated. Flipping through a volume, I would stop at pictures and decipher the captions.

I would read: *The California Condor is almost extinct*, wondering what *extinct* meant. So I would look it up in the dictionary to fully understand the context of the caption. (Years later when I learned the species had been reintroduced in the western United States, I felt a knee-jerk surge of nostalgic joy.) There was another encyclopedia in the library called *Childcraft*, much easier to read and chock-full of glossy pictures. When you opened a volume, a good smell came out, the enticing aroma of a new book.

Equally fun was the pictorial dictionary in several volumes that I discovered in the section for education majors. I was always attracted by pictures associated with instructions: how to crochet, how to knit, how to fold origami animals. And so I whiled away the hours, my research satisfying my natural curiosity about countless subjects, eight hours a day, five days a week, from the end of June to the beginning of September. And it helped improve my reading comprehension. Not to mention my trivia IQ.

But there's only so much knowledge you can cram into a brain, so when my father finally showed up at the end of the day, I was ready to go home. But he often had other things to do, like use one of the enormous keypunch machines. We'd have to stand in line behind other graduate students to run his deck through the machine. If the cards worked, fine. If they didn't, he'd have to figure out which card in the keypunched series was wrong, then stand in line again to rerun the batch to see if it worked. Sometimes I'd be waiting in the library until 8:00 p.m. or even 9:00. I would go down to the lower level and find my dad still fussing over his cards.

"Dad, I'm starving." One time I asked him, "Aren't you hungry?"

And he said, "No, if you get busy working on something, you forget you're hungry."

So we wouldn't get home until after 9:00 p.m. My mother never said anything about our late hours. And by that time, even her greasy cooking tasted good.

For second grade, I had to attend a public school in my neighborhood. For as white as Timmerman was, A.C. Moore Elementary boasted the colors of the human rainbow. It was also diverse from a socioeconomic perspective as well. About 80 percent of the kids there were children of construction workers and lower-class families who lived in Henley Homes and another nearby housing project, Rosewood. The rest of the students had parents who worked at the university; their families lived in middle-class neighborhoods, in nice homes with two or three bedrooms. It was pretty easy to tell the two groups apart. The kids of academics generally spoke clearly and knew many more words than the housing-project kids. They also seemed to have better attention spans and definitely had better lunches. That was my first inkling that financial means could be more of a factor than skin color when it came to getting ahead academically.

Two of the middle-class girls, Ellen and Janet, were very nice to me. Janet's mother drove me in her station wagon during a field trip. The other passengers were daughters of professors; listening to them converse with Janet's mother and among themselves was a revelation. I hadn't known that family life could be so peaceful, civil, and interesting or that socialization could be comforting instead of competitive.

In class I was very serious about my studies and did just what I was told. Math was easy, thanks to the workbooks my mother had given me. But reading remained a challenge, and I had to work very hard to get the hang of it. My goal was to be teacher's pet, and I always was. I wasn't the smartest, but I was the most compliant, and I loved being the teacher's favorite in every grade. I was growing up as my mother's English-speaking right-hand man; teacher's pet was a step up from that. And it was more fun than writing out your parent's bills.

In 1972 there were no after-school programs, no child-care centers in my Columbia neighborhood. Most women were housewives, or they worked nearby and could come home to take care of their children after school. My mother had to leave home at 6:30 a.m. to catch the bus to work, returning home twelve hours later. My father studied numerical analysis by day and worked the graveyard shift at the Magic Market convenience store. If they didn't make some kind of arrangement, I would be a latchkey kid, a thought that made me nervous.

Beyond the attempted theft of our car and my father's

pilfered underwear, other incidents convinced me danger could be around the corner at any moment. One of the other Taiwanese ladies who lived in our complex—she was the wife of a graduate student—told my mother about an encounter she had walking home to her apartment a few days earlier.

"A man started following me, saying: *Hey, girl. Hey, girl.* He kept following me up." She said it freaked her out so much she just started running. Then he started running after her until she made it to her building and the safety of her unit.

That story really made an impression on me, and I became hyper-aware of my surroundings. I wasn't worried about any particular race or ethnicity. I was on the lookout for anyone exuding malice or ill-will. And that included spies from Taiwan. This concern didn't come out of left field. I had been raised by parents who believed they were constantly being watched by pro-Nationalists who kept eyes on Taiwanese immigrants. I suppose the worry was they might try to start an opposition party from afar, so the government wanted to identify potential dissidents.

At that time Chiang was known for cracking down on any group that challenged him. Word was that anyone who spoke out or became too vocal would get a cautionary letter in the mail from Taiwan. The government knew who they were and what they were doing, even halfway around the world.

So my father and his circle of friends were very aware of anyone who spoke Mandarin (as opposed to Taiwanese), especially if they were graduate students. Mandarin was not spoken in Taiwan until 1949 when Chiang Kai-shek declared the language compulsory in all schools. For people growing up during my parents' time, it was forbidden to speak Taiwanese in public; you could speak it only at home, and very secretively at that. Even now, Mandarin is the official language of Taiwan, which is why there was an almost innate suspicion toward anyone speaking that language.

I know it seems hyperbolically cloak and dagger—or *hanfu* and *jian*, if you will—to assume we were surrounded by international spies, but that was the reality back then. In order to stay Switzerland and not project any political leanings, we would attend the Chinese New Year festivities put on by the Mandarin-speaking students as well as the autumn festival.

My mother was surprisingly into the Chinese New Year and had me put on a skit every year. That first taste of applause was like a drug, and I lost all my shyness performing in front of others. But my dad would freak out. *Quit putting her onstage. They'll do something to us.* His attitude was that the best thing to do was keep your head down and avoid doing anything that could be construed as subversive.

So that was my world view in second grade. The world was a complex, dangerous place. But it was also about to get a little less lonely at home. My brother was born in 1971 in an old county hospital, typical of the 1970s South. The tall building was made of dark, old bricks and probably dated back to Prohibition. This inner-city hospital was like a smaller version of Bellevue. Wards were furnished with eight rows of beds. The only privacy offered was a curtain you could pull around each bed. But it was better than giving birth on the kitchen floor.

The custom back then was to bottle-feed newborns. Breastfeeding meant that you were poor, so it was a prestigious thing to bottle-feed. Our welfare plan gave us free Similac and Enfamil—stacks and stacks of formula that took up a significant portion of the living room.

In Taiwanese culture, babies and children aren't cuddled the way American parents do. As a kid growing up, since we only socialized with other Taiwanese families, I didn't think it was unusual. There were a handful of other Chinese families at Henley Homes, and they didn't bestow much affection on their children, either. It was normal; I didn't feel that I lacked for anything or was missing out. But then after I started school I saw how physically affectionate American parents were with their children. And how okay and happy the kids were about it. So when my brother was born, I treated him the same way, cuddling him the way I did my favorite doll.

Because my brother was born in the middle of December, my mother had one week off for maternity leave plus one week for Christmas and New Year's. That was it. We needed to find babysitting for my little brother. There were a lot of stay-at-home moms at Henley Homes, so we went door to door soliciting for babysitters and found one. My mother would drop him off in the morning and then pick him up after work.

I had my own babysitter because my requirements were different. Once I started second grade, there was no more carpooling like when I had attended Timmerman, so my mother wanted my babysitter to have children around my age so I'd have someone to walk to school with. There was a row of apartment buildings near the Piggly Wiggly, and that's where we found my first babysitters, the Chavis family. I loved them all. There was Mrs. Dorothy Chavis, her husband Junior, and the grandmother, who slept in a big, high bed in the front room. The Chavises had an odd, unemployed maternal uncle who lived down the street in another one of the low-income houses. Uncle Jed was a scrawny, unkempt guy. He was always looking for a job and never finding one, but he was good at fixing things. And there were three kids. Doris was in fifth grade, Bubba, the only boy, was in third grade, and Jenny was in first grade.

Even though I was terribly shy, I looked forward to getting dropped off there every morning in the pitch darkness. I absolutely loved being in these people's homes. The atmosphere was lively with children, activity, and conversation. I soaked it up. The Chavises even had a cat, which fascinated me because we never had any pets.

Mrs. Chavis always treated me like one of her own kids. Soon I was devouring collard greens, black-eyed peas, hominy grits, biscuits, okra, fried chicken, and corn bread. It took me no time at all to prefer authentic Southern food to my mother's home cooking. The coolest thing at the Chavises' house was watching TV shows—great programs like *Gunsmoke* and *Bonanza*—with the kids and Grandma in her living room-bedroom combination. Their old TV broadcast in brown and white, not black, but we didn't even have a TV, so I was delighted.

Like their mom, the Chavis children included me in everything. I wasn't yet a street kid like them, but I was determined to become one, and fast. Bubba and Jenny gave me a dime of their own money to buy my choice of delicacies, either a pickle or a lemon, at the neighborhood Piggly Wiggly. But we had to get there, and that meant crossing a busy street. I learned how to look back and forth, and then became a pro at crossing the street. I was proud of my accomplishment. After that, we went to Piggly Wiggly every single afternoon. Going was the best part of the day.

I spent all second grade and half of third grade with the Chavises, and then they moved. I can't remember the reason they left, but neighbors where we lived always tended to be transient. Just like we were. So with little notice, we needed to find me a new babysitter. Instead of walking from door to door, my parents and I got in the car and drove down the street very slowly. We were stalking, looking for kids who lived there. The two girls on the sidewalk looked about my age, seven going on eight. They were walking along, jostling each other while bouncing a tired-looking Spalding ball. The sibling resemblance was obvious.

My mother told my father to stop the car so I could talk to them.

"Where do you live?" I called to them through the open window.

"Over there," one of the little girls pointed across the street to a house on stilts, around the corner from where the Chavises had lived.

"What grade are you in?"

"Third."

The younger sister said, "Second."

"Do you think your mom could babysit me after school?"

A third girl joined them. She was older, maybe eleven or twelve, and walked with a tween swagger. "What's going on?" she asked in a tough sort of voice.

"Does your mom babysit?"

"Well, we have the same mom. We're all sisters."

My parents and I parked in front of their house and went to talk to their mother, Mrs. Cushing. By the time we left, I had a new babysitter for one dollar a day.

By nature I was on the shy and quiet side, but the main reason I didn't talk much at first with the Cushings was that it was hard to get a word in. Theirs was a chaotic household. The girls fought all the time. For punctuation, they slammed the doors every day, all day, even in the morning before school. Every door in that house had chipped paint and stress marks around the edges.

Mrs. Cushing's three daughters—Terrilyn, Ellie Mae, and Charmaine—were the picture of sweet femininity. Until they opened their mouths. To them swearing was a sport, and when out of earshot of their mother, they were on the varsity cussing squad. And I was their very willing student. I think they found it amusing to hear a string of happily expressed obscenities flow from someone who looked like an exotic doll.

They weren't nasty, just good-naturedly foul-mouthed. Their turbulent and anarchic lifestyle wasn't going to change just because a visitor was in their midst. For any reason, or for no reason, they would shout out a *goddam motherfucker*, which sounded like *Gah damn mutha fockah*. *Go to hell* turned into *Go to hay-ell*. Then they would slam the door for effect.

These houses were very compact, with everyone crammed together. You walked in the front door to the small front room, then through the second room, which was a bedroom, and through that to the all-in-one, which was a combined kitchen and dining room. If you kept on walking, you'd be out the back door. That was it for living space.

For the first two months, I sat quietly on the front room sofa. Finally I spoke. "Excuse me, excuse me, I have a question."

The hubbub hushed. They were shocked I was capable of speech.

I meekly asked, "I've been trying to look this word up in the dictionary, and I can't find what it means."

They waited expectantly.

"What does motherfucker mean?"

They all shrieked with laughter, holding their sides, throwing their heads back, repeating my question between gulps of air, all three girls rolling on the floor. I can't remember if I ever got my definition. But that day marked my assimilation into their bizarre family. They'd been nice to me until then, never mean, but I felt more included after that. I ended up laughing with them.

Terrilyn told her sisters, "Y'all need to watch your dirty mouths, you muthafockas."

I learned that swearing in America isn't just used to express anger or frustration. It's a unique form of communication among certain cultures and groups. While *motherfucker* can be an expletive, it can also be an adjective, adverb, good thing, bad thing (depending on the inflection) or an expression of surprise. Perhaps it was a logical extension of Americans' tendency to wear their emotions on their sleeves more than Asians in general and Taiwanese in particular. But if you want to fit in somewhere, it can start by adopting the lingo. So by the time I was seven, I had the vocabulary of a salt-crusted merchant sailor. No matter that I didn't really know the words I was repeating or their (various) meanings yet; it made me feel like one of the girls. It also made me feel more American.

While I walked to school with Charmaine and Ellie Mae, I didn't always walk home with them. I don't remember why; I just recall on those occasions wondering how I was going to get safely from school to their apartment. The solution came in the form of Lisha Thomas,[1] the toughest tomboy I'd ever met. We weren't in the same class; she was a special needs student. Looking back, I'd guess she was both emotionally and developmentally challenged. But she adored me. It's not like we went through the traditional dance of getting to know each other through playground small talk.

We met because I had a problem. I needed someone to walk with me from school to the Cushings' apartment. Remember, to me at that time danger lurked around every corner, from weird guys following you home to Chinese spies. I had noticed her at school because other kids were leery of her. First, she was in the special-ed class. Also, she was very tall and big for her age and wasn't very talkative, so she presented an imposing figure to your average six- to eight-year-olds.

So one day after school I was dreading the idea of walking home alone and saw Lisha standing at the fence throwing rocks at something or someone. I walked over to her.

"Lisha, are you walking that way?" I pointed.

"Yeah." She kept hurling rocks, which I found oddly comforting—here was a girl who could defend herself. And by extension, me.

[1] Her name has been changed to protect her privacy.

I asked if she would walk with me and she agreed. From that moment on she would appear, my self-appointed protector. Whether because of my size or my deference to others in social settings like school, Lisha felt she needed to look out for me beyond keeping me company going home. It was like her calling. If anyone inadvertently bumped into me on the playground, she would body them up and tell them to move along.

Despite her loyalty, I can't say that I was really friends in the usual sense with Lisha. We never really played together or visited each other's homes. I knew she lived somewhere in the Henley Homes project, but I have no idea what building or unit. Still, in my child's mind the person I kept company with, even for a short time, was my pal. I would feel very connected to specific individuals in my environment, like the cussing sisters or Lisha, the special needs girl who protected me in second grade. And in my time around her, I also saw she had a really sweet side to her. Her physicality was just a defense mechanism to minimize people making fun of her.

I didn't walk home with Lisha every day; just when the babysitter's kids weren't there for whatever reason. But she was always there watching out for me on the playground.

I settled into a routine during the school year: to the babysitter's in the morning, school, back to the babysitter's to wait for my mother to pick me up. So anything to break up the sameness was always welcome. Even though my mother had a job sewing undergarments, she didn't earn enough to bring us above the designated poverty level, and my father didn't work for most of the year because he was a full-time student. That's why we qualified for the low-income housing and food stamps. So you had to budget your food carefully. But every two weeks a truck came to Henley Homes, which generated a lot of excitement among the kids because they would hand out loaves of bread, butter, cheese, flour, and other items. It was like a kitchen pantry Christmas. I have no idea who sponsored the truck, but it was a bit of excitement to break the routine and meant some extra meals. I was too young to see it as a handout or a reminder of our downward mobility. That would come later.

Chapter 4

發現

As a kid, all I knew was that Lisha Thomas was in a special education class. I don't know what condition she suffered from, but I wouldn't be surprised if it were a chromosomal abnormality. She was developmentally delayed but way too tall for her age. People—adults as well as kids—avoided her because she acted strangely and looked off and not so subtly dangerous. But I wasn't afraid of her.

Although she was as big as an adult, she talked like a five-year-old—simple and completely without boundaries. What she lacked in vocabulary, she compensated for in strength and fearlessness. She was tactile, always wanting to touch me. She often talked about her genitals. Now I suspect that someone in her environment was molesting her, but back then something like that wasn't on my radar. I just sensed she was lonely and didn't have anyone her age pay attention to her. With Lisha by my side, I knew I was safe on the playground. We met each other's needs perfectly, so on that level we became very good friends.

Mother would come pick me up at the Cushings' house at around 6:30 p.m., very predictably; her bus was quite punctual. She would appear outside the front door and wait. She never knocked or stepped inside. I'd open the door a few minutes before the bus was scheduled to arrive and watch for her through the screen door. If I weren't ready, one of the girls would come and get me.

One afternoon I was in the middle of a vocabulary lesson with Charmaine when my mother arrived.

"Shit," I said. "This goddamn hellhole." We weren't fighting; I was just practicing my swearing.

"No, no," she coached me, all her vowels drawn out in that distinctive Southern drawl. "It's SHEE-it."

Through the screen door, I saw my mother and gestured that I was coming.

"Okay, try this," Charmaine said, winding up the lesson. "Git back home, you li'l motherfucker," she said in a pleasant, conversational tone.

As I stepped outside, I turned back to Charmaine and said sweetly, "HAY-ell, you're the ugliest li'l motherfucker."

As we walked away, I looked back. Charmaine and I smiled and waved at each other. I couldn't wait until the next day.

Eventually, the Cushings would also end up in my life's rearview. And again, I don't remember why. My last babysitter in Columbia was more qualified. Miss Hartman was a school crossing guard. Her daughter, Teresa Hartman, was in first grade when I was in fourth, but there were only two years between us, and we got along well. Every afternoon we turned on the TV and watched *Match Game* and *Family Feud*. *Soul Train* was another one of Teresa's favorites. Watching the black kids dancing on *Soul Train* is how I first learned to dance—at least in my mind I was dancing.

Teresa's big sister did not approve. She didn't think whites should emulate blacks. I suspect her attitude went far beyond dancing. When she came home, she'd yell at Teresa: "Ya'll turn off that nigger music!"

Remembering her comments now shock me. At the time I didn't realize just how inflammatory her comments were. The N-word was spoken freely by many whites and some blacks in my environment. I never copied that. Even as a youngster I instinctively understood it was often spoken with a tinge of hate or disdain. It wasn't playful. I also learned from Teresa's sister that when you were around white people, you didn't want to dance like blacks. You didn't want to do anything "black" around white people. Things were very segregated in South Carolina, even in the 1970s.

৯

Because my mother never talked to any of these babysitters, she had no idea what I did every morning and afternoon in their homes. Neither she nor my father ever asked me how my day went. Nor did I volunteer any information. There was no real reason not to, except that I was possessive of that time; I felt it was my American time, and that was a learning curve my parents had no interest in. And when I swore or mimicked the kids I hung out with, I didn't sound Chinese. I sounded like my surroundings.

Bilingual children are everywhere in our multicultural society, and their mastery is impressive. My two languages were fluent, but my mastery of both was mediocre. Even as a little girl, I didn't consider myself bilingual because I knew I wasn't grammatically proficient in either language. My English was limited to what I picked up from all those babysitters and from the street kids who were my companions. School didn't help much; I was ahead in math, but never caught up in English and reading.

As for Chinese, I could not understand even ordinary Taiwanese news programs. I still can't. My spoken Taiwanese is conversational, not formal, and it's limited to basic words and phrases; complex expressions might as well be ancient Greek. As an adult at a Taiwanese seminar, I had no idea what the higher-level speech was about. In a Taiwanese church, I couldn't grasp the main idea of the sermon or decipher the hymns.

You hear stories of how immigrants would watch TV to learn English on a rudimentary level—*Sesame Street* being a favorite. But my mother never sat down to even try, always too busy doing ... something. My father and I, and later my siblings, watched for entertainment and had many favorites: *Mission Impossible, Hawaii 5-0, Cannon, Kojak, Streets of San Francisco, Barnaby Jones, Hart to Hart*—basically every cop and detective show there was.

My mother would walk by and complain. "You're all learning bad habits from that. Look how awful their manners are, how they talk to adults and each other."

At USC in Columbia, most of the graduate students' wives took a free course in English as a second language offered at a local church. My mother enrolled and tried to learn English. She would carry a dictionary around and write the Chinese pronunciation next to the English words, but she never gave her studies the effort that was necessary and quit after just a couple of weeks.

In that respect, I was lucky. It's in my DNA to do whatever it takes to accomplish a task if doing so will better my situation. My mother was never like that, and her attitude kept her from living the fuller life she could have had if she'd been more adaptable.

Her first job in the United States was at Stone Manufacturing Company, where she sewed bra parts and men's underwear. She later worked at Columbia Uniform Company, embroidering patches on uniforms and caps. She didn't complain about the monotonous work because she knew her limitations and did not want a job that required English conversation. Her work was straightforward: here's your task, follow instructions, do it this way. You don't have to ask questions; you just do. Punch in, punch out.

Obviously learning a new language as an adult is difficult, but millions of immigrants before her had done it and established successful lives. It was almost as if she viewed her time in the United States as a temporary stay.

And her unwillingness to assimilate, or at least learn functional English, put additional responsibilities on me. In our household, translation was like a bottomless pile of laundry that's never finished. My parents handed me every letter, every bill, every correspondence that needed to be answered. That's not a typical household chore for a fourth grader. I was game and did my best, but I really wasn't equipped to know which car insurance company we should buy or how to juggle what bills to pay. I did whatever my parents asked, so my evenings were always tied up with forms, letters, and translation instead of homework or playing with my baby brother.

The irony is that while my spoken English was fine, I was still behind in reading. You'd have thought all this extracurricular practice with my parents would have helped, but it didn't. Nor did my early education in the public schools of South Carolina improve my reading comprehension or correct the bad grammar I picked up from other kids. Even as an elementary school student I could see the glaring differences in education between Timmerman and A.C. Moore. The bar was undeniably higher in the private school and the attention given each student more focused.

The teachers seemed equally dedicated, but from classroom size to available materials to infrastructure, everything seemed weighted in the private school's favor. It was easy to see how from a young age a kid's perception of their place in America could be informed dramatically differently just by where they went to school. In a country with so many divergent ethnic and racial backgrounds, a uniform playing field when it comes to education seems crucial to maintaining a level playing field for opportunity and achievement. Not to put too fine a line on it, but my father's grammar was better than mine, which tells you all you need to know about my elementary public school education. But it was instructive in other ways, such as the unique way American boys flirt.

I never felt any racial discrimination even though I was a tiny Chinese girl a year younger than my classmates. Most of my classmates had never seen Asians in their lives. That's not an exaggeration. According to the 1970 census, the demographics of South Carolina were 69.3 percent white, 30.4 percent black, and .3 percent other, which included Native Americans and Asians.

In fourth grade, most of my classmates were black kids. One boy, Bruno, would sharpen his pencil more than he needed to because my desk was next to the pencil sharpener at the front of the room. I always sat up front because I was so tiny. While there, he would always touch my hair or tap my shoulder and then pretend that he hadn't. It seemed like he had to sharpen a pencil every five minutes. It wasn't the hair touching I found annoying; that I understood. I was fascinated with the black kids' hair—Afros were the latest fashion trend—and had an urge to touch the soft explosion of hair. It was the tapping.

When I complained about it, the teacher suggested he was simply trying to get my attention. To me it would have been easier just to say something. The next time he came to sharpen his pencil, I smiled shyly and quietly giggled a little. Then after a while he stopped teasing me. I was glad the tapping had stopped, but I realized later I didn't mind the underlying attention.

Whether it was because I had an exceptionally thick skin or an exceptionally sunny outlook, slurs never bothered me. Such as the time a girl in class named Catherine said, "My brother talks about Chinks."

Not that I knew what that really meant, but you could sense it wasn't complimentary. Even so, I still went to Catherine's house anyway when invited. She wasn't discriminating against me; she was just repeating what her older brother had said. To me, that was all just conversation. It didn't mean that she didn't like me.

Sometimes kids would call me shrimp, which I thought was a cute nickname. I didn't think I was being ostracized. If someone was going to take the time to call me something, I liked the attention. They didn't call me ugly names like monster or gorilla. I thought they were trying to connect with me, get on my wavelength, bond with me. By coming up with nicknames, I thought they wanted to identify with me, to find common ground. It was always joking; it never turned mean or ugly or xenophobic. This is not to say that bullying doesn't happen. It clearly does, and it's a serious problem that can leave kids despondent. I'm just saying I never experienced it, although looking through the prism of today I would have seemed a prime candidate. Perhaps it was because everybody at Henley Homes and A.C. Moore felt like outcasts, so we were all in the same boat.

And even if kids were teasing me, it didn't rise to the level of upsetting. I actually enjoyed that childish interaction. I felt special. A lot of time was spent standing in line—for lunch, for an assembly in the auditorium, to come in from recess—and kids get restless. When the kid in front of me would do something funny or weird to me, it made me feel like a popular kid. Their antics were entertaining and it was often the only child-to-child peer interaction I had all day.

I am acutely aware that the current atmosphere toward immigrants is less than charitable in some quarters. Maybe I'm looking through the rose-colored glasses of memory, but it didn't seem as much of an issue back then. And it's not just about illegal immigrants but all immigrants. Life was hard enough just struggling to find footing; having to face animosity based solely on the fact you weren't born here would have made life much more difficult.

For as much as I was all in about assimilating, one area not high on the list was church-going even though living in the South you are surrounded by churches. When I was growing up, my family didn't practice any religion. We didn't believe in God. We didn't even believe in any kind of higher being. But we didn't believe in not believing either. That's pretty much the definition of being agnostic.

The first time we went to a Christian church was in Rock Hill for a potluck dinner. It was a community thing that someone must have invited us to. The next time we went to a church function was in South Carolina. One of my father's classmates invited us to an all-you-can-eat pancake supper at his church. The people were pleasant, but I suspect my parents went for the free meal.

Even though my parents were not believers, they did let me go with a third-grade classmate, Sandra, to Sunday school at her Baptist church. I'm not sure they understood it was a religion class. After going a few times, the girl and her parents—her dad was a house painter—suggested we stay for the service. I said okay because I was told we'd be given a little piece of cracker and some grape juice. I had no idea that I'd have to sit through a five-hour service for a snack. And unlike the famous AME churches, there was no great black choir—which makes sense since it was a white congregation—nor was there any music at all.

My parents didn't like me being gone that long so after that I was only able to attend Sunday school. But I stopped going not long after. If the idea was to convert me, it fell short. I was no more a believer after Sunday school than before.

Henley Homes eventually became just too dangerous and shady, so we moved a few blocks away to a cramped duplex on Oceola Drive. That's where we were living when my sister Mingfang was born in April 1975, when I was in fourth grade. With three children and two adults, we were uncomfortably cramped in the tiny duplex that was only about eight-hundred square feet. One night, I overheard my parents talking about moving again, and I hoped it meant moving into a bigger space. But what it actually meant was leaving Columbia. My father had failed the verbal defense of his thesis and had decided to go to a new program. So once again, we were pulling up stakes to pursue my father's quest for a PhD.

In my father's mind Birmingham, Alabama, was going to be our permanent home, so we were going to do the move right. He hired a mathematics grad student to drive the rental truck containing all of our belongings to Alabama. Alan, who was African-American, was older than most of the other students. He asked if he could bring along his eleven-year-old nephew for company in the truck, and my father agreed. Both were very quiet and mild-mannered.

During the long drive to Alabama, my father drove us in the car, with Alan following in the Ryder rental. We were largely traveling through small towns. We stopped for gas or bathroom breaks twice. At the first gas station, Alan—who was very dark-skinned—did not get out of the truck, although his lighter-skinned nephew did. I thought it was peculiar that Alan did not get out along with everybody else but assumed maybe he just didn't need to use the restroom. The second time, I knew that something wasn't right.

When we reached Atlanta, Georgia, the first major city we'd passed through, Alan sprang out of the truck and sprinted to the restroom like a one-hundred-yard dash track star. We all got snacks and supplies while I tried to figure this out.

"Why didn't Alan get out at the other stops?" I asked my parents. One good thing about having a private family language was you could say things that other people around you wouldn't know was about them.

"He's black," my father explained. "It wasn't safe earlier in those smaller towns. Something bad could have happened to him."

My mother added that it was dangerous for a black person to travel through small towns in South Carolina, Georgia, and Alabama. It was safer for him to stay out of sight in the truck. In Atlanta, an urban area, he was okay. As for his nephew, people wouldn't bother young kids, so it was all right for him to go out and bring back supplies. This was in December 1975, and there were still areas where it was dangerous for a black man to be. The unfairness of it all made me feel even worse about moving.

After we'd moved our things into the new apartment, we turned in the Ryder truck, and then my father and I drove

Alan and his nephew to the Birmingham airport so they could fly home. We had paid him cash to drive us there, and we paid his airfare home. Flying home was safer for them than taking a bus home that would travel through areas that might put Alan in danger.

Sitting in the front seat with my father, with Alan and his nephew in the back, I couldn't help but worry. It didn't matter that he was educated, kind, and good. He was still a dark-complexioned black man. And for that it would not be safe for him to ride a bus back through Alabama and Georgia. The idea that there was such hatred out there based solely on the shade of someone's skin made us just as vulnerable as Alan and his family.

On the way to the airport, we passed through a poor area in Birmingham, with cheap wooden houses packed tightly together.

"Those are typical black homes," Alan told us. "You can pour water through a window in one house, and it will hit the floor in the house next door."

Father and I went inside the terminal at the airport and waited with them until they boarded the flight home to Columbia. We thanked them again then went back home and assured my mother they were safely on their way.

She looked up from the box she was unpacking with an audible sigh. "Oh, I am so relieved."

We all were. And that was the last we ever saw or heard from Alan. But the experience stayed with me. I learned that some minorities or anyone targeted for hate or bias, like Alan, sometimes believe they have to stay in the shadows to avoid conflict in order to succeed.

But I think seeing Alan's fear planted a seed within me not to live in the shadows no matter where I was. And for the most part, nobody can accuse me of staying out of sight. As

I've freely admitted, I love the spotlight, so from going for my medical degree to years later auditioning for the Dallas Cowboys Cheerleaders, I have a tendency to be out front and center. So what was true for Alan was not true for me. But then again, I did not face the same discrimination that he did in that place at that time. While we might not be able to cure others' prejudices, we can choose how we respond to them.

Chapter 5

發現

*B*efore we even unpacked I was homesick for Columbia. I missed Lisha; who would keep her company? I missed my teachers and the attention they gave me. I also missed my last babysitter, Lynn. I felt very connected to specific individuals in my environment, whether adults or children my age, and Lynn was one of those people. She was a single mother who went to bars at night and came back with a different man every day. She would tell me about her troubles, and I considered her my close pal. When we moved away, I worried what she was going to do without me. From earliest childhood, I learned from my father to seek the best about any person or place. To this day I can find good things to appreciate about the worst person in my environment—the most annoying neighbor, the rudest salesperson, anybody. There's always a bright side.

On moving day, I had been practically immobilized by feelings of loss. My father was also feeling sad. Honestly, it wasn't that Columbia was so wonderful—we were poor, we lived in a cramped apartment, our neighborhood was economically depressed, and my father seemed to be spinning his academic wheels. But it was familiar. The old Devil you know phenomenon. And the thing about change is that while it sometimes might improve your lot, sometimes it could make it worse. Plus, my parents had developed their Taiwanese circle so once again they found themselves completely isolated. My mother didn't understand why we were reminiscing and torturing ourselves. My mother was more pragmatic; life was what it was, so moping about it was wasted energy.

In January 1976 after the holiday break, in the middle of fifth grade, I showed up for my first day at Avondale Middle School in Birmingham. Being the new girl in school was hard, I think especially so because I was homesick. It had been easier to move when I was younger. The older you get, the deeper the roots you plant.

My classmates in Alabama were more advanced than those in Columbia in reading, which was still my Achilles heel. I was beginning to think English comprehension was genetic and that maybe Asians weren't wired to read English. I still had to read by using my finger along the sentence and reading word by word. It was slow and laborious. It was also frustrating to see how quickly my classmates were able to read. In retrospect I suspect I have a reading disability of some type although I've never been tested. It wouldn't have occurred to my parents. And I doubt it would have occurred to the school system. They probably just assumed my problem had more to do with being an immigrant than some physiological condition, even though I was raised in the United States.

The bright spot at school was that within three or four weeks I became teacher's pet. For as behind as I was in reading, I was a whiz in social studies, and I was way ahead in math. More to the point, I was attentive, polite, and while quiet I always tried to have a cheerful demeanor. And I was a hard worker and determined. Reading disability or not, I've always been a compulsive reader. It would just take me longer, but I never let it stop me from achieving. I have an insatiable appetite for knowledge—always have—and teachers picked up on it.

Even though I came to this country as a two-year-old and am very American in many ways, I suppose my philosophy of life is more Chinese in that I never assumed I would get opportunities. I was taught that I had to earn and create my own opportunities. You're not entitled to anything, so you have to work harder than everybody else. Not only wasn't there a term for work-life balance, it wasn't even a concept worthy of pursuit. There was no room to worry about happiness, only achievement.

We'd been in Birmingham only a month, and my mother still hadn't found a job because she didn't speak English. She'd been trying to find some kind of assembly plant job. But job hunting wasn't easy because my mother still didn't have her driver's license. I often wished she did because at least she would remember to pick me up on time, unlike my father, who was chronically late.

But nothing compared to the time in Birmingham when he literally forgot me. I waited after school for hours. There were no cell phones to call, and we did not have a phone in our apartment, so I had no way to reach anyone. I was still waiting when the last kid had been picked up. Still waiting when the teachers had all left. Still waiting when the janitor locked the school and gate.

He finally showed three hours after school ended. He offered no excuse of a meeting running late or having to finish a lab. He admitted he simply forgot about me. By this time he had already flunked out of two PhD programs. My parents never complained about their lot in life. And my father was too busy chasing his dream to complain. He just couldn't get his act together. They couldn't even pick up a kid from school before the janitor closed for the night at 5:30, hours after the other kids had gone home.

He was very quiet on the way home that night, lost in thought. Looking back, I think that was the day he suspected Birmingham was not going to work out. Three weeks from the day he forgot to pick me up, he was ousted from the graduate program at the University of Alabama. Either he was booted out, or he left before they could kick him out. He had not even started his course work. I was told to tell anyone who inquired that the field of study didn't turn out to be what he'd signed up for.

With no prospects in Birmingham, my parents decided to move back to Columbia by default. They didn't know what else to do or where else to go. Eight weeks after we'd left, we returned without fanfare. We found a furnished apartment that first day at the Kilbourne Court. The big news about that apartment is that for the first time we had a proper closet.

My father returned to USC although I'm not sure doing what. My mother found a job at Columbia Uniform Company sewing patches onto uniforms and embroidering employees' names onto the shirt pockets. I was back in the same town and the same school with the same friends. Lisha and I resumed our connection as if I'd never left. The time in Birmingham took on a dream-like quality. As if we'd been abducted by aliens but instead of losing hours we had lost months.

In times like these, my father often found solace in music. He had a record player and was partial to guitar music, Bluegrass, and songs like "Tennessee Waltz." I didn't have a musical preference back then. Nor was I exposed much to popular music, which is why our visit to one of my father's acquaintances in graduate school. His name was Nathaniel. He was black, and he was married with a son about my age. It was the first time I'd ever been in a black's person's home. I'm not sure what my nine-year-old brain was expecting, but it was just like any other home I'd been in. The only difference was the occupants' skin color. Funny how a superficial difference makes us assume so much else must be different between us. And yet we don't assume people with blue eyes are inherently different from brown-eyed souls. Forty years later and I'm still trying to figure that one out.

When we got there, Nathaniel's kid asked if I wanted to go listen to some of his records. I said sure. We went to his room, and he played the Jackson Five. And I remember thinking how cool it was because it had a great beat. The stuff my dad liked was so slow it could put you to sleep. My dad said he liked listening to "Tennessee Waltz" and similar songs because it helped him think. I liked music you could dance to.

Our mutual interest in music is what led to me playing the cello. The University of South Carolina had received some government grant to promote music in underserved areas. The professor running the program would assign graduate students to work with local kids. They came to A.C. Moore looking for kids who wanted to play a stringed instrument. The graduate student would then teach you thirty minutes a week in a group lesson. USC would loan students the instruments.

I wanted to do this and showed my parents and my father was very supportive. The problem was the lessons were on the USC campus. My school was over at 3:15 p.m. and the lesson was at 4:35 p.m.

"But Papa, how am I going to get from school to the lessons?"

"Well, I'll take you."

My years of experience to the contrary, I chose to believe him and signed up. My father took me to the orientation session on a Saturday morning. There were four graduate students, three men—one played the bass, one played the violin, and one played viola—and a pretty young Korean woman who played the cello. At the end of the orientation, you got to choose which instrument you wanted to learn.

I was leaning toward the violin. But my father seemed mesmerized by the cellist, who kept swinging her hair as she played. He said, "Pick the instrument that lady is playing," so that's the only reason I chose it. My dad picked a cello because of the pretty Korean cellist. Why would I want to do the cello? I was tiny, and the instrument was taller than I was. And you have to brace it between your legs. It was like doing the splits sitting down.

My father did take me for the first lesson but was late picking me up. Miss Kim, the graduate student, would announce: "You're twenty minutes late."

I'd apologize and try to explain, but she didn't want to hear it.

"You know, this is a thirty-minute lesson. When you are twenty minutes late, you have ten minutes left to do that. At this point do not even take that cello out of here, just sit there."

I was so humiliated, so embarrassed being tuned up by the teacher. I know that's why now I'm early to everything. I ended up getting driven there by the parent of another kid from my school who was also taking the lessons.

I started taking the lessons at the beginning of fifth grade. Then we moved to Alabama, so I missed the next semester but started back up in sixth grade. Miss Kim had me audition for a small, beginner's orchestra. You had to do that once a week. I did pretty well with that so she had me audition for the higher-level orchestra and I made it. I was so thrilled. Those rehearsals were on Saturdays. The kids in that orchestra were so good I couldn't keep up. Initially, they'd put me at third chair, but I couldn't keep up, so they bumped me back a couple of chairs, which was fine.

By sixth grade I was taking the bus to school and to practice, no longer dependent on my father or the kindness of classmates' parents. The upside: I was always on time. The downside: I couldn't take my cello home to practice. I kept it in a locker where we rehearsed because it was too big to carry on the city bus. Not practicing at home meant I was never going to be first or second chair. But that was okay. I had no dreams of being the next Yo-Yo Ma. Just being part of the orchestra was good enough for me. Again, I found fulfillment just by being included. In being part of something bigger. In being accepted as just one of the gang.

But that's the thing about being an immigrant or the child of adult immigrants: you live a dual existence. In your mind you are American. You were raised here, absorbed the culture, view this as home. But inside your house, your parents' culture often holds sway. Ideally, the two sides comfortably coexist and enhance each other. You can love your adopted country without it diminishing your reverence for your heritage.

In my case, my heritage was often shrouded in hushed tones and almost a sense of mystery. My parents were clearly proud of their Taiwanese roots, but they were reticent ever to celebrate it. They were too afraid. It was a fear most Americans at the time could not fathom although in the political climate of 2017, there may be more empathy for their dilemma.

Even though we were often on welfare, my father saved money like crazy. From his first day in America in 1966, he was very frugal. When teaching math at Prairie View A&M in Texas and Friendship College in Rock Hill, he squirreled away a little bit from each paycheck. While we lived in Columbia, he taught at Voorhees College during the summers and diligently took money out of each payment and added it to his savings. One reason he accepted the rent-free trailer at Friendship College was so he could add that saved money to his stash.

Saving was his mission, and the money was earmarked for one purpose alone: to take our family back to Taiwan, where three of us were born, for a visit. He was very attached to his parents and siblings, and his distance from them pained my father. The separation was made exponentially worse because of the restraints put on communication by the then Kuomintang government led by Chiang Kai-shek.

When my father left Taiwan in 1966, he didn't imagine that it would be ten years before he would see his relatives again. During that time his father had died, and his family was placed under surveillance because my father had left for the United States. He also had a fear that he might be in physical danger returning to Taiwan.

The repressive regime that my parents left behind was always in the background of our lives. After my mother and I had left in 1968, she too had limited contact with her family for almost a decade. They didn't speak on the phone. Besides the expense and that we often had no phone, there was also a likelihood that the calls would be monitored and recorded by the government.

Aerogrammes—blue, lightweight one-page letters that you folded in thirds before mailing—were the only form of written communication permitted by the Kuomintang regime. Regular letters in sealed envelopes were not allowed and would be intercepted in either direction and discarded by the Kuomintang.

The Kuomintang would steam open every single aero-gram and verify that its content was sufficiently bland and innocuous before allowing it to reach its destination, which is why every aerogram that arrived in our mailbox never contained anything newsworthy or emotional. My parents' letters to their families were equally superficial. *We're doing fine. How are you?* Nothing personal, no emotions. Just basic facts that could not be misconstrued. And photos were never exchanged.

The Kuomintang regime was violent and unpredictable. Until Chiang Kai-shek died in 1975, the only time you could speak Taiwanese, even among family members, was behind closed doors. If anyone outside heard you speaking anything besides Mandarin, you could be thrown in prison and executed by a firing squad. Mandarin was the only language taught in schools.

As much as my parents, especially my father, longed to see their homeland, many fears kept us from going until after the dictator's death. And even then, my father obtained his American citizenship before the trip; otherwise, he very likely could have been detained and not allowed to return to the United States.

There were other reasons he was nervous to go back and visit. He had left Taiwan specifically to earn his PhD in the United States. After getting his master's in mathematics back in 1967 at Mississippi State University, his academic pursuits had stalled. He didn't want his family to know that. He was embar-rassed to return home without having achieved his main goal and needed to save face.

My father decided that when his relatives in Taiwan asked how things were going, he would simply say he was still working on his studies. His Taiwanese relatives were not very educated, so they would not know how long it should take to pass a verbal defense and a written defense of a thesis, then to write the dissertation, and then defend that.

Taiwan might have been my native country, but it was completely unknown to me. I'd spent all my formative years in the United States and considered myself American. I was traveling to a new world and had no idea what it would be like or how it would change my perception of myself.

Chapter 6

發現

We flew to Taiwan on July 4, 1976, America's bicentennial. Looking back I wonder if my father was aware of the irony: returning to a country still traumatized by the years it spent under a dictator's thumb on a day celebrating democratic freedom.

My siblings had never been on a plane, and I obviously didn't remember the trip over with my mother eight years earlier, so the experience was new to me as well. My sister, fifteen months old, was able to fly free if she sat the whole time on someone's lap, so my parents and I took turns as human booster seats. My brother was five and a half and would have fun wherever he was. He was fascinated by the gadgets and loved looking out the window at the clouds below. For me the trip was an opportunity to explore my native land which was a complete foreign country, so I spent the hours traveling anticipating what it was going to be like.

I had a lot of time for my musings. We flew from Columbia Metropolitan Airport to Los Angeles, where we caught a thirteen-hour flight to Guam and endured a six-hour layover until our flight to Tokyo. Feeling jet-lagged and grubby, we arrived four hours later at the glistening Tokyo International Airport. The first thing that struck me as we disembarked into the terminal was that for the first time in my memory, I was surrounded by Asians in public. No one stared at us or regarded us as anything remotely special as we headed toward the gate for the flight to Taipei. All around us, people were bowing to each other in varying degrees of deference.

In the United States I'd have the occasional Chinese classmate, but for the most part I was the unique, exotic one. Here I was just another unremarkable face in the crowd. It was a jolt. Being different had become the norm for me. It informed my identity. In this crowd of Asian—mostly Japanese—travelers, you'd think I would have felt like I had come home. Instead I felt off balance, an oddity. I felt like a minority.

From the time we left South Carolina, it took nearly thirty hours to reach Taipei, Taiwan. We were greeted by a group of five or six happy, smiling relatives who of course were complete strangers to my siblings and me. There was my widowed paternal grandmother, her son who was called Second Uncle on the father's side in Taiwanese. English is a much more direct language—Aunt Li Na or Uncle Zhang just seems so much easier—while Taiwanese has a complicated system with different names for maternal and paternal aunts and uncles, and everyone is ranked by birth order. So because I was the eldest, all the cousins on my father's side addressed me by the same respectful title my brother used, Big Sister. No relatives called each other by their actual names. Introductions could take a while.

In the United States the arrival of long lost relatives

would prompt an affectionate, noisy scene with everyone hugging, touching, kissing, and crying. In Taiwan, it was as if we had just seen them that morning for breakfast. My parents and the relatives who came to pick us up were muted in their hellos. No affectionate gestures, no excited chatter. I got a bigger reception from my teachers at school on Monday mornings. Viewed through a ten-year-old's eyes, my relatives seemed underwhelmed to meet me. I understand now that's just the way the culture was, and still is. But it just added to my sense of not belonging.

Other relatives had traveled with my grandmother and second uncle, driving more than two hundred miles from my father's home village on the southern coast of Taiwan to Taipei. Many of the roads they had taken were little more than country lanes.

Second Uncle and my grandmother had reserved two rooms for that night at a nearby hotel—the five of us in my family in one room and all the relatives in the other. It was a generous gesture. While they weren't starving, they were far from wealthy, unlike my mother's family. In fact, other than the four round-trip plane tickets, we spent zero money while we were in Taiwan. We didn't have to pay for any meals because everybody fed us. We didn't pay for any lodging because our relatives put us up wherever we went. From their perspective we belonged to them, and they took care of us accordingly. From my perspective the jury was still out.

These new relatives might have been strangers to me, but I could see a physical family resemblance between us. But they were so different in personality from my parents that they might have come from an alien civilization.

During the drive to the hotel, my grandmother and father talked nonstop, trying to catch up on the past decade in an avalanche of words. The rest of us wouldn't have been able to get a word in even if we had wanted to. There was so much news about my father's brother, two sisters, and father that my grandmother had felt she couldn't share with him via phone or letter. This was news that could only be safely told face-to-face.

Many of her stories centered on political harassment. Not long after my father had left for the United States, government officials stopped by his parents' house every so often to check up on activities.

"What are his intentions?" they asked.

They showed up regularly at first then as time passed the visits tapered off. I wonder now whether that anxiety was a factor in the stroke that killed my grandfather. He was an unsophisticated, self-taught car mechanic, and even if the family had nothing to hide, such encounters had to be stressful and intimidating.

It was fascinating to me that my father's travels would be the focus of so much interest. But then again hardly anyone from Nahpee ever ventured to America. Taiwan had been under martial law since 1949, and people had learned not to attract attention in any way. The restrictive Kuomintang regime, which probably should have been paranoid about uprisings since they were so hated, was the main reason my father left. But he wasn't part of an overthrow plot. He simply wanted a PhD so he could live a more comfortable life and enjoy the prestige that came with the achievement.

The Taiwanese are big on giving and getting gifts. The minute we got into our hotel room, my mother plopped her suitcase on the bed and snapped it open. Even the most everyday American items were considered highly-prized luxuries.

Procter & Gamble products were very scarce and popular, so my mother gave my grandmother and second uncle tubes of Prell shampoo. Never mind that the stuff turned your hair into straw; the bright-green packaging elicited a chorus of *oohs* and *aahs*. My mother also doled out Avon toiletries, such as face and hand lotions, to all of the relatives.

My paternal grandmother was very nice to me, but she absolutely adored my little brother. In traditional Chinese families having a boy was quite frankly more important than girl offspring. Hence the very real phenomenon of infanticide of baby girls in mainland China, which instituted a one-child rule to try and hold down population. In 2010 the United Nations reported that among youths nineteen and younger, there were twenty-five million more males than females. Another study in 2003 estimated there were forty million girls born who were "missing."

Fortunately, Taiwanese families didn't go around drowning their baby daughters. But they prized boys just as much as the mainland Chinese. And usually much was expected of sons. That's one area where my parents broke the mold, primarily because of being immigrants. They relied on me more because I knew English and was the eldest child. But even when my brother was old enough to assume some of those duties, they didn't ask him to. Since my parents never showed preference for one child over another, it was eye-opening to see my relatives fawn over my brother. And just *thismuch* annoying.

My brother of course reveled in the attention. He was a typical five-year-old: happy and goofy, jumping up and down, running around. He wasn't shy at all with the grandmother he had just met, and he made everyone laugh by walking all over her feet and running circles around her. Grandmother thought he was the cutest thing ever. She spoke to him in Taiwanese, but he apparently had no idea what she was saying.

Or pretended not to. Instead of responding, he kept saying cookie, his favorite food group. That was practically all he said during the entire trip.

Some bilingual children are slow to become fluent in either language. This made for some Who's on first? moments. He once took Grandmother's hand, said cookie—as in: *Let's go find some*—and led her out of the hotel room. But *cookie … cookie* sounded like a Taiwanese phrase that means: Keep going, keep going. So my grandmother walked up and down the hall with him, asking: But where are we going? He of course didn't understand a word she said, so he kept leading her along asking for cookies.

My brother hardly spoke any Taiwanese, but even if he had, he wasn't much of a talker. For a boy who would grow up and attend Harvard Medical School with distinction and complete two residency programs, he was practically mute until he was eight or nine. It didn't take long for Grandmother to offer my parents some unsolicited advice, telling them they needed to pay more attention to my brother.

"This boy, you've got to groom him, get his education up to par. I know that the daughter here"—that would be me—"she's all right. But you've got to work on this kid. After all, he is a boy."

It was clearly understood that because he was a boy, he was compelled to succeed. My father appeared to listen thoughtfully, but I could tell that my mother did not appreciate the parenting suggestion or the subtle dig of her mother-in-law's comment.

My father's farming and fishing village was called Lin Pien in Mandarin Chinese and Nahpee in Taiwanese, which has no written characters. Nahpee is on the coast in Ping Tung, the poorest county in Taiwan even though it enjoys some of the most fertile soil and ample fishing in the entire country. Nahpee is renowned for its seafood, and the residents proudly told us—over and over—that "we are number one in seafood."

But it would be a while before we arrived in Nahpee. We were off to see the country. After a much-needed night's sleep, our family took a train the next day from Taipei to Taichung, a city about a hundred miles south along the western coast. Second Uncle and my paternal grandmother came along. We all stayed overnight at my adopted great-aunt's house in Taichung. My paternal grandfather had one brother and no sisters, so his family had adopted a girl.

In my grandparents' time, if you had children of only one gender, you would informally adopt a child of the other gender from some nearby relative who has several children of each and then raise the child as your own. So technically my great-aunt was not a blood relative, yet she was very gracious to us and generous, offering enough food as if we hadn't eaten in days.

The next day we left my father's family behind and took an impromptu trip to see my mother's side of the family. We traveled one hundred miles on a sooty steam-engine locomotive along the Western coast to Tainan City, where both my mother and I were born. The trip took forever because the train stopped at every city along the way.

My mother had not seen her parents since 1968. They were in their eighties by the time of our visit but still very healthy, regularly climbing six flights of stairs to a rooftop terrace, where my grandfather tended an impressive bonsai garden. My maternal grandparents and all of our relatives treated us wonderfully. I met my mother's only brother—called Uncle on the Mother's Side. Our cousins took us to a beautifully landscaped park and bought us lots of Orange Fanta, which was all the rage in Taiwan. We drank that every day; it was everywhere. It's a wonder everybody wasn't a raging diabetic with as much sugar as they regularly consumed.

My maternal grandparents' house—my very first home as an infant—was opulent but missing amenities I took for granted having grown up in the United States. For example, I was fascinated by their toilets. You couldn't flush toilet paper; the canal was too small. They didn't have refrigeration, either, so they bought vegetables at the outdoor market every day. Food was stored in a cupboard and quickly consumed before it could go bad.

Both my grandmothers were fastidious housekeepers. I attribute this to the Japanese education they received when Taiwan was under Japanese occupation. My parents' generation, growing up during the regime of Chiang Kai-shek, was nowhere near as neat and tidy. Both grandmothers' hair was always combed perfectly in place, and their homes were spotless and organized with almost military precision. Even though they were older and slower with poor posture that bent their bodies like question marks, they rose early every morning to tackle their daily regimen of work and activities.

During our stay in Taiwan, we regularly traveled back and forth between my parent's hometowns, apparently to give both sides of the family equal time, attention, and respect. There didn't seem to be a predetermined plan; it always seemed rather impromptu. And not very time efficient, even by a ten-year-old's perspective. The trip between Tainan city and the village of Nahpee took half a day each way because of all the stops. When my father was enlisted to help decide what should be done about his younger sister's illegitimate child, my mother refused to be part of that family business and stayed in Tainan while my father traveled alone to Nahpee.

The two different sides of the family were a study in contrasts. Just like my parents themselves. The old saying: The apple doesn't fall far from the tree was probably coined about a Taiwanese family. While the trip to the homeland was primarily for my parents to reconnect with their families and cultural roots, it also gave me context for why my parents were the way they were. Why my mother seemed resentful toward my father and disdainful of our surroundings no matter where we lived. Why my father –against all rational reason—kept trying to push the PhD rock up the mountain even though it seemed clear he'd never make it to the top, rather than finding a decent-paying job teaching high school math somewhere so his children could enjoy a middle-class life with permanent roots. And he could stop killing himself on this quixotic academic quest.

Obviously, the finer points of understanding my parents came later as an adult with a career and family of my own. But even as a ten-year-old, I saw my parents in a new light after meeting their respective families. I might not have been able to pinpoint in words what it all meant, but I was certainly able to appreciate the emotions of it. I think it was starker for me because unlike most kids who grow up with extended family around, this was the first time I had ever seen either parent in the role of a child and all that entails in an Asian family even when an adult. I also saw them in their natural element, the relationships and dynamics that had molded their personalities.

The first thing that surprised me was how luxurious, by comparison, their upbringing had been compared to what my siblings and I were used to. My mother's family, the Wangs, were decidedly middle class, which in Taiwan is considered privileged. Over the years I've come to believe that accounted for her attitude when facing our financially trying circumstances. Her family was financially secure when she was growing up, so she never developed the skill set to handle the adversity she experienced in the United States while my father pursued his PhD.

Her father was a retired soybean merchant who ran a prosperous business located on Yung Fu Road, a very busy street in Tainan City. My grandfather's clients were café and food store proprietors, and he did well enough to support two families in style: His first wife had died, leaving him with four sons. His second wife, my maternal grandmother, had five children. None of his children struggled or lived in poverty, and all were educated. My maternal grandmother was also an educated woman for her time. She was a midwife; in fact, she delivered me in a home birth. Midwives were more highly esteemed than nurses at that time.

Tainan is a cosmopolitan city that attracts many tourists. Established by the Portuguese and the Dutch, it's the oldest city in Taiwan. One of the more popular structures is Chihkan Tower, originally a fort built by the Dutch in 1653; in 1875 a sea god temple and pavilion was built on the site after the fort had been destroyed in an earthquake. Within its grounds are statues, ponds, and an assortment of buildings known for their classical Chinese architecture. There are baby pictures of me taken at Chihkan Tower.

My little brother and I loved our maternal grandparents' house because it was our own tower—a six-story home great for kids to explore. It was built like a narrow stack of blocks, with only two rooms on each level, which were connected by steep flights of stairs. The first floor was rented out to people who ran a business. My grandparents occupied the rest of the building. On the second floor were a living room, dining area, and kitchen. The third, fourth, and fifth floors were bedrooms. The terrace and garden were on the sixth floor.

My grandparents slept in separate rooms, following an Asian custom that it's not proper to be seen in the same bed together even if married. Intimacy occurred after the rest of the family had gone to sleep, then it was back to their respective rooms once the encounter ended. Not exactly the stuff of Hollywood romance.

The house was beautiful, but in retrospect it was a dangerous place for children to play. Even my parents—not what you'd call safety-first types—commented on the dangers of the terrace garden; The ledge all around was so low that even adults could easily fall over onto the street below. And all the bedroom windows—of course unscreened—remained wide open, day and night. The window ledges were low enough that my brother or I could have easily climbed up and fallen out. I was a glass half-empty kind of kid, so I made sure my siblings stayed away from the open windows.

Leaving the windows open also meant letting in an assortment of lizards, mosquitoes, and other flying insects, and even the occasional bird. But if you closed the windows you'd likely suffocate. The weather was so humid, and there was no air conditioning. The open windows also meant you were constantly bombarded by the noise from the busy street, and a film of soot would accumulate on the furniture from local factories. God only knows what our lungs looked like breathing the polluted air.

On one hand the pollution and close spaces seemed like a worse way of life than our modest surroundings at home, even though my grandparents' tower home was considered deluxe, even palatial in Tainan. It was just one of the many cultural disconnects the trip exposed.

After visiting with my maternal relatives and experiencing their upscale lifestyle, we were back on the train to Nahpee. Technically, even though I was born in Tainan, by

Asian tradition my father's place of birth is considered his children's hometown regardless of where they were physically born. And as it happened, in many ways I connected with my roots in that simple farming village far more powerfully than I ever did in the opulent bustle of my actual birthplace, which in turn gave me a clearer perspective on my American identity.

In 1990 my family returned to Taiwan to spend time with family. My maternal grandmother is on the left; on the right wearing the pearls is her sister, my great-aunt.

Visiting one of the oldest Buddhist temples in Taipei while rocking my pink sneakers. It's a Taiwanese tradition to light incense in temples and ask for good luck, good health, and for their children to get accepted by a top university—not necessarily in that order.

During a January 2015 working trip to Taiwan, I attended a traditional Chinese opera in Sanxia. The woman's costume reminded me of the clothes my grandmother used to send me when I was growing up. And you wonder why people thought of me as a China doll ...

Celebrating a birthday at Henley Homes Day Care/ Kindergarten program in 1970. Party hat notwithstanding, I don't look very happy to be there.

Fourth grade at A.C. Moore. The three other girls and I were selected to be library monitors. Kind of ironic considering I was always so behind in reading.

Class photos were invented to keep an orthodontic visual history of your youth. Lost my first tooth while at A.C. Moore. The bottom photo was taken in first grade at Timmerman when I was five. The yellow ensemble was courtesy of my maternal grandmother in Taiwan.

My father's mother surrounded by her grandchildren. I'm in the brown top sitting on the concrete bench, second from the right.

My father and his siblings in 1990. He's in the middle. This is the only picture I have of them all together. Next to my father is Oldest Aunt. Looking at them standing side by side—talk about separated at birth.

My maternal grandparents relaxing at home in 1976.

After thirty years of marriage, I finally met my husband's paternal aunt during a 2015 trip to Taiwan.

A typical food stand— Taiwan's version of fast food. The streets are filled with people, exhaust fumes, the cacophony of traffic, and the irresistible aroma of spices and hot grease.

From 1972 to 1974 my father taught summer school at Voorhees College in Denmark, South Carolina so I spent many days hanging out on the campus.

Whenever my parents got into an argument while we lived at Henley Homes, my mother would take a time out by walking me to this local diner that was bustling in the 1970s. She'd order French fries but be too angry to eat so I always got the entire plate. For a long time I got to have fries at least once a week.

Chapter 7

發現

Even though the first person to greet us at the airport was my paternal grandmother, we went to spend time with my mother's family first. I'm not sure what family politics were playing out between my parents and their respective families that determined who we visited when, but my father's mother didn't seem to mind that we went to Tainan first. She seemed thrilled when we showed up in Nahpee to spend time with her.

My father's parents lived in a very modest two-story house, but they were no worse off than anyone else in their village. They had provided their five children with food, shelter, and an education. Their home when we visited was full of energy and warmth. They weren't as well-to-do as my mother's parents, but by Nahpee's standards they were middle-class.

When we got there, my father and all his relatives went outside, while my mother and I unpacked. The silence inside was interrupted by sharp popping noises coming from outside.

We ran outside and saw two of my uncles setting off fire-crackers. I was surprised and confused to see my mother start crying.

"This is a very big deal," she explained, wiping away her tears.

"Why?"

"Because they're so happy to see your father; they're celebrating because he has come home."

So apparently in Taiwan, visiting relatives was akin to celebrating national independence in the United States. The display seemed unusual to me because I'd never known my immediate family or any of the Taiwanese families we visited in South Carolina to be particularly demonstrative. My father's youngest brother, who we called *Youngest Uncle on the Father's Side*, set off some more fireworks, which were attracting a small crowd of excited neighbors.

My father, who I knew as an affable but largely disengaged parent, was apparently a local Nahpee celebrity for having traveled halfway around the world in pursuit of his PhD. I was amazed that his return would prompt a holiday atmosphere. Of course, nobody there knew of his struggles and certainly my parents weren't about to destroy the illusion. So his relatives were effusive in their pride. Nobody else in my father's family had ever left their little coastal fishing community in southern Taiwan. During the entire decade he'd been gone, only two other villagers had summoned the courage to leave Nahpee.

Just going to the United States was a major achievement and no one in my father's family had ever gone to college much less earned a master's degree. So there was a lot to be proud of. But my father had hung his reputation on getting a PhD, so he felt he had to keep up appearances or risk disappointing not just his family but the village.

Another reason my father had left was you couldn't qualify for top jobs unless you joined the Nationalist Party/ Kuomintang. My father was hired as an assistant professor in Taiwan, but he wanted more. While I may not have appreciated his choices as a ten-year-old, now as an adult I can, even if I disagree with his refusal to reassess once it was clear Plan A wasn't viable. But the concept of saving face is deeply ingrained in most Asian cultures.

We stayed at my paternal grandmother's home for more than a week. Second Uncle, who had come to the airport with Grandmother to pick us up, lived on the main floor with his wife and three young children. Third Uncle, his wife, and their three school-age children lived on the second floor, and Grandmother slept up there too. They all cleared out their rooms to make space for the five of us.

The whole family shared one minuscule refrigerator on the second floor that had a lock on it. I'd never seen a locked refrigerator before. I found out the lock prevented my cousins from taking food needed for meals because only a few essential ingredients could be refrigerated in such a tiny space.

The second floor where we slept was one space separated by flimsy wooden partitions into three large bedroom areas. The partitions provided little privacy, and there was only one overhead light so if one person turned it off, everyone was in darkness. And instead of a bed as I knew it, there was a huge wooden platform raised several feet off the ground that was big enough for five or more people to sleep in. There were no sheets, pillows, or mattresses. Wealthy people slept the same way, except their platforms were made from more expensive wood.

Sleeping on a wooden board was not comfortable, but it made the climate more bearable. Taiwan is hot and humid, especially on the southern coast, so you don't want a mattress or any kind of cushion under you that would just become sweat soaked, which in turn would attract gnats and mosquitoes. Given the alternative, a plain wooden platform didn't seem so bad.

Every night at bedtime was an adventure. Kind of how I imagined camp would be like: a free-for-all. Family members would lay down anywhere they wanted, jostling for position. They would hang netting for children and babies to keep them safe from mosquitoes. But it got ridiculously hot under netting, so you had the choice of covering up and broiling or get bitten all night long and risk getting mosquito-borne diseases like dengue fever—something I'd never had to worry about in South Carolina.

Exhausted from traveling, we fell asleep early. I was awakened at dawn the next morning by what sounded like barking dogs, someone walking down the road hawking their wares, and cowbells. Toto, we were definitely not in Kansas anymore.

My paternal grandmother's house was on a two-lane road. Literally. There was no sidewalk or lawn, so when you stepped out of the house, you were on the road. Every morning Third Uncle unlocked and lifted a wide, metal roll-up door, which exposed my grandmother's living room to the passing world. Everyone's home in Nahpee was like that. The door was left open all day, and anybody could walk into your living room anytime, but people usually didn't. However, lizards and geckos were frequent guests. But they ate mosquitoes, so nobody minded them.

In the afternoon Grandmother would go to the terrace above the second floor to heat up huge buckets of bath water over a wooden stove. Even though she was in her sixties, my grandmother lugged the buckets downstairs to the second floor by herself. Did I mention that my grandmother, my two uncles, and their families—eleven people in all—shared a single bathing and toilet area on the second floor? Then add my family and you had bathroom gridlock. Everyone bathed in the afternoon because if you waited until nighttime, the water would be cold.

It was the first time in my life I'd been in a house without indoor bathroom plumbing. You bathed by standing in a pan and ladling water over yourself. I would never take a shower for granted again. Or flush toilets. Inside a closet in the corner of the bathing area was a kind of pit toilet—basically a hole in the floor you squatted over. But instead of the human waste going into the ground as with an outhouse, it went down a chute to a sequestered area on the first floor. Then early every morning someone came by to collect the waste from each house, load it onto a truck, and drive it away. That's how sanitation worked for everyone in the village and surrounding towns. I was pretty horrified by it all because it was just so unsanitary.

After taking my "shower" and getting dressed, my clean hands had to touch the door latch that everyone had handled after using the chute toilet. There was no sink or faucet in there; in fact, there was nowhere on the whole second floor to wash your hands. The only sink was in the kitchen, where they were cooking. I stood there as clean as could be under those conditions, not wanting to touch that latch. Finally, I lifted it with my elbow.

And my relatives lived in what was considered a very nice home for Nahpee. To say I was in culture shock was putting it mildly. The one thing that was familiar was the cooking. Dinner included white rice covered with a greasy pork sauce.

It was the kind of typical Taiwanese meal my mother usually cooked, so I was prepared for that.

But that was the only thing my parents had prepared me for. I guess it didn't occur to them how alien this experience would be. Nor did they try to help me adjust because they were too preoccupied with family dramas to notice I was shell-shocked. My father was embroiled in his sister's affair and her illegitimate child; my mother was too busy fighting with her mother-in-law over butting into her sister-in-law's situation. My grandmother finally announced to my father: "She's not part of this family. She needs to stop advising us."

In the United States in-laws are considered part of the family, but in Taiwan, there is a definite line drawn in the kinship sand.

One of the things I liked about Grandmother was that she was very tidy and clean with a well-kept appearance. She was proud of her home and washed all the floors every day, dusted the furniture, polished the stove, and wiped down all the wooden beds every morning. Grandmother was warm and kind to me although she never once hugged or kissed me. In fact, during our entire visit neither grandmother touched my parents or me. I was used to that and didn't think anything of it. Keeping your emotions to yourself is so ingrained in the culture, especially with the older generations, that when we took pictures with all of our cousins in Nahpee, nobody even smiled in any of the snapshots.

Many years later, my brother and I started hugging our parents in the American manner when we were leaving home or returning for a visit. They were practically horrified and would just stand there motionless, not knowing what to do.

But it felt more natural to us than bottling up emotions, good or bad.

On our second day there, my uncles' wives took me out to the market. They were very warm and inclusive toward me, which made me feel like part of the clan. Second Uncle's wife held my hand while we shopped for fish and vegetables. Whether it was from affection or fear that I would get lost and she'd be responsible, it made me feel very close to her.

Several of my aunts asked if I ate Cracker Jacks, which I thought was odd. I later found out there were a lot of Americans in Taiwan during the 1960s and 1970s. The United States had a military base on the island until 1979, and when on leave the soldiers would hand out boxes of Cracker Jacks to kids, which made them very popular. I guess from that they assumed all kids in the United States must like Cracker Jacks. But I didn't know if I liked it or not because I'd never eaten any.

After we returned from the market, I wandered upstairs to admire the little shrine set up in a small parlor near the bedrooms. Above a table with incense were sepia-toned portraits of my dead grandfather and his father. The tradition was to burn the incense on special occasions, such as my father's homecoming. It's not a religious-based ritual; it's a sign of respect for ancestors. I knelt down and studied the portraits, trying to think about my grandfather and great-grandfather, but it was hard to do because I'd never met them. So instead I started thinking about my grandmother and how casual she was acting toward the son she hadn't seen for more than eleven years. It was obvious that she had really missed her son, but she was reserved and never overbearing. Even though she clearly favored my brother, I was grateful for the warmth she showed me.

The display reminded me of some Buddhist altars I'd seen, but not nearly as elaborate. Not surprising since I knew that my father's family was not religious. They didn't believe in a Christian God. They didn't follow Buddhism. My mother's family was even less spiritual. There were no memorials to any departed relatives anywhere in the house, no photos to sit near and contemplate. They didn't even have incense in the house, which considering the sanitation system's lingering odors would have been very welcome.

However, one day I was out with my maternal grandmother and near her house was a well-known Buddhist temple. She asked if I wanted to go in. I did. We went inside, and I was struck by how quiet it was compared to the busy street we'd just been on. The churches I had been in were on the gilted side, but the temple was very unassuming. Outside there were trees and a modest yard. Instead of one main area, it had a series of connecting rooms where people could go meditate or pray. In the back there was a nice garden and classic-style old wooden bridge. We just walked around then left.

It was easy to see why my parents were agnostic. My father was especially pragmatic, convinced there was no higher power. It was up to people to do what they needed to do. I was still thinking about that when my Grandmother came up the steep stairs and stood next to me. She looked at the photos of her late husband and father-in-law then down at me.

She said, "This is your home."

Even as a young girl, I knew she was not speaking literally. Obviously, my home was in the United States. I was more American than Taiwanese in outlook and attitude. I was fluent in English, only passable in the language of my parents. But what I understood her to mean was that wherever she or my relatives were, I would always have a home. She was speaking about the essence of family, which transcends language, geography, years, and even DNA; the place you know you can go and be welcomed and taken in unconditionally.

It's not about responsibility as much as honoring the ties that bind, the shared ancestors and history that connect us across generations.

I was both touched and melancholy. Even as a child I could never envision living with my parents when I was married with children the way my uncles and their families were living with Grandmother. Whether because I was "Americanized" or because without the influence of their families, my parents had become too self-involved—my father with his academic pursuit and my mother with her resentments—to instill those threads of family bonds into their children. We were a family although in many ways we lived separate lives. But kneeling in front of those photographs beside my grandmother I felt a profound kinship that went deeper than blood.

She struck a match and handed it to me so I could light the incense. Through the tendrils of smoke, I looked up at my grandmother, trying to memorize her face, her perfectly combed hair, her kind eyes. In one week, we'd be on our way back to America. There was a good chance I'd never see her again.

Good thing Taiwanese have a strong sense of family because we were freeloading off every relative my parents had. We'd stay at one house then move to the next, securing unlimited room and board in exchange for a green tube of Prell shampoo and Avon hand cream. Our hosts were uniformly gracious, but there were times I sensed we were overstaying our welcome. Well, not *we* as much as my mother. When she was around my father's relatives, she turned into a diva. She acted as if she was superior, which visibly irked some of my father's kin. The irony was she lorded living in the United States over them, even though when there she acted miserable. I realized it wasn't America she disliked; it was not living in the relative style she had grown accustomed to with her parents. I guess the reason she put up with my father's academic transience was that his PhD was the ticket to the standard of living she expected.

My mother was generally snarky about other people, but her disdain for my father's side of the family was a nonstop litany. "Your paternal grandmother is not very educated. Look at her over there; she is not very sophisticated. Your father's side is poorer than we are. They don't have very good provisions." On and on and on. Even her body language could be haughty and disdainful. You'd think that someone in my mother's position would have been humble. Unlike my father—who never acted like he was better than anyone else—she'd never attended college and only worked at low-level jobs. She refused to learn English or how to drive. She might have been happier as a person if she had given her in-laws a chance.

Even at my tender age, I had often been around uneducated people in different environments—specifically, my babysitters. Most of them were not educated. But you can always learn something from anybody, educated or not. For example, the Chavises taught me about white and Southern culture and cuisine. And through their love of *Bonanza* I also learned a little about the Old West. And my friend Janine would teach me things that are still part of me. These kinds of interactions give daily life substance and enhance your own humanity. Don't think my mother ever learned that.

The tension between her and my paternal grandmother was obvious. My mother made clear through her expression, tone, and body language that she emphatically did not like her mother-in-law. I got weary of the nastiness, but of course it wasn't my place to say a word. Sometimes I wondered how and why my parents ever got married since my mother so clearly felt his family was beneath hers—and her.

I'd later find out their marriage in 1965 had not been a love match. When my father was a graduate student, he earned money tutoring math. One of his students was a young lady who had become friends with my mother after they met in a ballet class. The student's mother introduced my father to her daughter's good friend, who at the time was in teacher's college. When my mother learned her friend's tutor was going to study in the United States, she saw an opportunity. So it wasn't a love story; it was more a practical agreement. The marriage was arranged between the families and quickly took place. My father was twenty-six; my mother was only twenty-four.

What happened next was me. My maternal grandmother pushed my mother to get pregnant as a way to further cement their marriage; she was worried my father might find a new, American wife. In other words, I was collateral to make sure my father didn't bail on the marriage. A little over a year after their wedding I was born, and my father left for the United States five months later.

With so many family members around during the early months of their marriage, my parents didn't get to interact very much. When my mother and I left for America, my parents hadn't seen each other for two years. They had to learn how to deal with each other without the buffer of extended family. To be fair, they had both been spoiled growing up, not just my mother, so compromise didn't come easily to either of them. They wanted what they wanted. But because of culture and circumstance, my father was in the position to make his wants the priority.

My father was the eldest living child in his family, followed by two brothers and then two sisters. The older sister—Oldest Aunt—became a family outcast after she married a member of the Kuomintang party. According to family lore, Oldest Aunt had not been a desirable match on the surface because she was quite unattractive with only an elementary school education. However, a selling point was that her older brother—my father—was a graduate student in the United States. Of course, people envisioned him as an Ivy League professor. Even so, the matchmaker's pool of suitors was limited. The man she married appealed to her because he had a college degree. It seemed unfair that the family matched her up with someone they knew was a Kuomintang party member then shunned her for marrying the guy.

But she ended up being the least of the family's problems. Youngest Aunt was having a heated affair with a married man. In addition to the children he had with his wife, the man also had an illegitimate daughter with Youngest Aunt. This was not what her family had expected. After elementary school, Youngest Aunt had applied to work as a tour guide. She had to pass an exam about the history, geography, and culture of China and Taiwan. The other requirements were reminiscent to those for flight attendants in the 1960s and 1970s: neat grooming, perfect posture, a pretty face, and a lovely figure. She checked all those boxes and was hired as a tour guide.

One day at work a guest "forgot" his camera on the tour bus. When he came back to retrieve it, he introduced himself to my aunt. They were soon embroiled in a love affair. Not long after, my little cousin, Chu-san, had been born. The little girl was a toddler at the time of our visit. My father and grandmother went to visit Youngest Aunt, but I wasn't allowed to meet her daughter—my cousin—because of the family's shame over the situation. I'm also sure being excluded was a way to express the family's displeasure.

The treatment of my father's sisters gave me pause. On one hand my grandmother stressed the importance of me understanding this was my home, and yet they had essentially disowned my aunts because the family didn't agree with their choices. My immediate family wasn't particularly complicated; this was my first experience with the drama of large families, and it seemed a bit suffocating.

My grandmother constantly fretted over what to do about her daughter. What they wanted was for the man to marry her. But he was a government employee who could not possibly afford to maintain two households. The fact he was already married was not the issue. At that time in Taiwan and other parts of Asia, bigamy was very common. If a married man had a mistress, he would often set her up in a home and support their children. Some men had as many as three separate families, which was accepted if they had the financial means to support them properly.

While Youngest Aunt's affair was not unusual culturally, it still brought shame to the family. And somehow, my grandmother blamed my father for his sister's affair.

"This was your responsibility," she announced. "You left the country. If you had stayed, this never would have happened. You would have overseen these things. Since your father died, you were supposed to be in charge."

Younger Aunt's boyfriend had bought her a house as an informal settlement, but he didn't pay any child support. A situation like this would never end up in family court because it would be too embarrassing for everyone involved. But my grandmother would not back down. She wanted the guy to marry her daughter. My father dutifully tried to persuade the boyfriend to give his sister a better deal although there wasn't much he could do to force the issue.

A few years after our visit, Youngest Aunt married a temple caretaker, and they had a child together. Chu-san carried the stigma of being illegitimate, but she was exceedingly bright, attended college, and became a pharmacy technician. She stayed in contact with my family and occasionally corresponded with me on pink Hello Kitty paper. She even came to the United States in her twenties and harboring no resentment, visited my parents for a few weeks. None of the cousins on my father's side got too far in education, but there was this brave, illegitimate girl who had graduated from high school—a major achievement—and even attended college for a while, becoming a pharmacy technician.

When I finally got to meet her, I was a professional with a family of my own and was taken by her sweetness and accomplishments. I found it ironic that she ended up the smartest cousin we had on my father's side of the family. All she needed was a chance. All that angst I witnessed as a child in Taiwan ended up being wasted energy, caused mostly by parental expectations. Ten years later, I would experience the same disapproval over some choices I made.

After three weeks it was time to leave. I wasn't looking forward to the long trip ahead of us. The good-byes were more emotional than the hellos had been. It was easy to get caught up in the moment because I sensed a certain finality. I had felt embraced and loved by my relatives. They gave me so many mementos to bring back. My grandfather gave me a plant, which we had to lie about at customs. Both grandmothers gave me some photos, which I placed safely inside a book that

I packed in my little carry-on bag. After a final round of good-byes, we boarded the plane.

It had been an exhausting three weeks, and everyone was worn out. The return trip seemed to pass more quickly. My father watched a movie and then fell asleep with my little brother on his lap. My mother and baby sister slept soundly in their seat. I opened my bag and took out the handful of snapshots my grandparents had given me. Already my time in Taiwan was taking on a surreal, dream-like quality because it had been like stepping out of your real world into an alternate universe.

For as long as I had been alive, Taiwan was an underlying, almost mythic presence in my life. My parents' reluctance to talk much about their families because of their political concerns had made it seem mysterious, and I had a romanticized notion of what life there would be like. The reality of it gave me a new perspective on my parents but also made me appreciate the United States in a way I never had before.

As it turned out, I would never see most of the people in those pictures again because that wasn't where my life was. While visiting Taiwan helped me forge a connection with my ancestry, my present and future was firmly rooted now in America, which was my home in the sense of where I belonged. And going forward I would embrace that destiny and assimilation both on my own and also with a little help from my friends.

Chapter **8**

發現

*O*nce safely back in Columbia, I saw my surroundings and life in a new light. I was glad my father had given my siblings and me the opportunity to meet my relatives. But I was even happier to be back home. It was more than the full-sized refrigerator, bathroom sink, and flush toilet although I'd never take any creature comfort for granted again. Traveling to Taiwan made me feel more American than ever. My future depended on staying in the United States. I resolved to work hard in school to make the most of the opportunities I had here. The idea of having to go live in Taiwan was unimaginable and more than a little scary.

My fear wasn't unfounded, free-floating anxiety. It had become clear during our trip that my parents considered Taiwan a Plan B option. My father had spent years meandering in and out of graduate programs and was getting nowhere. If his despair ever outweighed his ego, he might go back. He could always use the excuse that as the eldest son he was responsible for looking after his mother and siblings. I could imagine him deciding if things didn't work out, we might as well all move to Taiwan. I made my own plans: excel in school, go to college, get my MD, and stay in the United States. Permanently.

What I discovered as a ten-year-old visitor to my native country, I still feel today: I cherish America's clean air, security, and safety. No democracy is perfect, each has its imperfections, but our political environment on a federal level strives for fairness and was designed to root out corruption through checks and balances. Everything is out in the open, and if our elected officials don't shape up, we can ship them out at the next election.

For all its social problems, there is still an overall sense of freedom in the United States that Americans really take for granted. This country, more than almost any other, is open to ideas. If you don't like one city, move to another. If you don't like city living, move to the suburbs, or go live on a remote mountain—nobody is tracking your moves because of who you voted for. You can be anything you want. You can express your beliefs. You can publish your book. Even the busiest cities have room to live comfortably. Conversely, Taiwan is very cramped in space and restrictive in freedom and ideology.

I'd been moved by how our relatives worshipped my father and celebrated his homecoming, but then again, if someone like him was such a hero, then their standards must have been pretty modest. I wanted to aim higher and was determined to work as hard as necessary to get there. I couldn't wait to start school to get on with the rest of my life.

But school was still a few weeks away. In the interim my father recruited me to help him with his dissertation. He had enrolled in yet another master's degree program at USC in Columbia, this time in computer science. His dissertation topic was the functioning of the Otis elevator system at the Thomas Cooper undergraduate library, which was all underground. At the time it seemed like a fine topic to pursue, but now as an adult I can see what a terrible research subject it was. He was testing something that had already been proved: Otis had done all the engineering and research necessary before building the library's elevator system, which started on the ground floor and went down five levels. Otis had already accounted for all possible permutations and combinations of floors, cars, and call buttons.

But there I was in the library helping my father test something that worked fine every day. He would have me run downstairs to a certain floor and push the button to see if the elevator came to him or to me. We did this for several weeks, and I thought it was very cool to be assisting with his dissertation project. I don't know what his conclusions were, but I do know he never got his PhD in computer science.

In August 1976 I started sixth grade at Hand Middle School. At 6:00 a.m. every morning my mother left my siblings and me with our latest babysitter. Cindy was a single mother who lived in our old neighborhood with her parents and two children. I never saw her without a cigarette in her hand or dangling from her lips.

Rather than pay for an after-school babysitter for me, my parents gave me keys to the apartment. For the first time in my life, I was home alone after school. The free school bus dropped me off a few blocks away from our complex. I would terrify myself when walking past a wooded area on the way home—make that, as I was running by it—about how someone could be hiding behind a tree or bush waiting to kidnap me. I wouldn't relax until I got to the Magic Market at the corner of our apartment complex and could see the cashier inside.

I didn't feel that much more secure entering our empty apartment all by myself. I got home at 4:00. By the time my mother took the bus home from work and picked up my brother and sister from the babysitter, she wouldn't walk through the door until around 7:00 p.m. I found being alone spooky but didn't complain to my parents. I never had homework, so the TV kept me company. I turned to the television for companionship. It made me feel safe hearing other people talk, even if they were just on TV. But my latchkey kid routine would change that October after an electrical short sparked a fire at Hand Middle School and left the building uninhabitable.

A few days after the blaze, the school let the students scavenge their lockers for any salvageable belongings. Cindy went with me, and as we got close it smelled like a barbecue gone way wrong. The contents of our lockers were set out on the scorched school lawn but what wasn't charred was water damaged or covered in soot. Nearly everything had to be thrown away.

A week later, the entire school population was relocated to the old Columbia High School. The long, empty building was huge and a bit intimidating. It was located in the center of downtown Columbia, right next to the Trailways-Greyhound bus station. The fire initiated a series of events that would change my life.

My new school was too far to walk home from so I needed transportation. I couldn't count on my father to pick me up. After forgetting me while we were in Birmingham and making me wait alone in the dark for hours, I swore to never again depend on him to drive me home. I could take the free public-school bus, but I'd still have to walk home alone from its bus stop through that creepy wooded area that scared me, especially as the days were getting shorter as we moved deeper into autumn. So I decided to take the city bus home. I didn't discuss it with my parents; I'd let them assume I was riding the school bus. I was determined to conquer my fears and master Columbia's public bus system without asking their permission.

I knew some kids routinely rode the city bus to school, so I went to the bus terminal after school, where a girl in my class explained I needed a bus pass. Students paid one dollar for ten rides, so I bought myself a card and tried it out.

The Trailways-Greyhound depot next to my school was the main transfer point for all of the city buses. I knew my mother took the Rosewood bus to her work. So after buying my pass, I waited for the Rosewood bus and held out my card for the driver to punch. The city bus was so much better than the school bus because it was full of commuters. When the bus reached my neighborhood, I pulled the bell cord and jumped off feeling jubilant. It took longer getting home using the city bus, but that was fine. The less time I had to spend alone in the apartment, the better.

Children who live in cities today commonly ride public transportation. Not just to and from school but to get around in general. In a place like New York, seeing kids on the subway and on buses—whether they live on the Upper West Side or in Harlem or Alphabet City—is part of living in a modern metropolis. But when I was growing up in the late 1970s, it was less common in a place like Columbia to see middle-class white kids on buses other than going to and from school. I don't know if that was because Columbia was a smaller city or because it was in the South. I know this because I started spending a good portion of my spare time riding buses around Columbia. Soon I was traveling all over town by myself. I'd often get off to explore an area I didn't know, which was most of Columbia. Not every part of Columbia was kid-friendly. Or people-friendly. At some of the bus stops, I was the only passenger who got off.

My travels were funded by one of my father's quirks: He didn't like loose change in his pockets. So when he came home in the evening, he let me have all the spare coins he had accumulated that day. Over the course of a week, it added up. He would also give me a few coins as a reward whenever I finished a section of whatever math book he had given me to work on. Again, I studied math all year long, including summers and school holidays, so I had that money stashed away as well.

Even though I didn't feel safe in all areas of Columbia even when riding the city, it didn't matter because I was free. That school year I roamed the bus system and the streets from 3:30 to 6:30 almost every weekday afternoon. While watching TV was fun sometimes, exploring my world was fun all the time.

The bus drivers started recognizing me—let's face it, they didn't have a lot of four-foot Asian kids riding their routes. Most were very nice. Some seemed to be keeping a suspicious eye on me. I'm sure they thought I was either a homeless orphan or a midget drug mule because I did not remotely look my age. I would also get strange stares from some of the riders because I looked so much younger than I actually was. I was going on eleven and barely looked seven. I also caught the attention of a girl I recognized from school. Janine Henderson[2] was a round, heavyset black girl who was in my science class. I'd find out later that she lived pretty far away from school. Her family had fudged and used her maternal grandfather's address so that she could go to A.C. Moore. So she needed to take the city bus to get to her real home.

The first time she saw me on the bus, she came over and plopped down next to me, bouncing me off the seat.

"Hey, girl?" Her personality had the force of a firecracker—startling but mesmerizing. "Where you goin'?"

[2] Her name has been changed to protect her privacy.

"Nowhere. Just riding around before going home."

"Sounds fun. I'll ride with you."

She talked pretty much non-stop, providing a running commentary on the other riders on the bus: someone with funny-looking eyeglasses (*I'd rather walk into walls than wear those ugly-ass specs*), pencil-thin people (*You know they don't own a fan because they'd blow over if they walked in front of it*), and mean-looking people (*That face would make my dog hide under the bed*). If passengers were rude, she would make faces behind their backs.

She was friendly and funny and acted like we'd known each other all our lives. By the time I got off at my bus stop for home, I felt like we were already friends. She filled a void I didn't realize I had—a best friend. Lisha had been my friend, but we never really talked; she provided a sense of security, not really companionship. Lisha also lived very much in her own head while Janine was an extrovert very much connected with the world. She embraced the day, even if it was just riding a bus. I didn't know the term at the time, but she was the poster child for carpe diem. Janine also came across confident and street smart—two things I desperately needed to work on. She was the yin to my yang.

From that first day on, she always wanted to ride with me. She teased me about being tiny, saying she was afraid I would get kidnapped by someone shoving me into their pocket, so she was there to protect me.

"Anybody want to mess with you, they gotta mess with me first." She reminded me of some larger than life sitcom character. "I'm gonna stick with you on this bus," she promised then teased, "It'll be like *Gulliver's Travels*, with you being one of those Lilliputians."

The literary reference was lost on me then, but I got the gist. She just adored me, and every day sharing a bus seat, riding through Columbia, we bonded and being around her made me see Columbia—and the world in general—more vividly, more colorfully. She also embodied the power of staying positive. If you believe you can do something, often you'll do it. If you choose to be negative, you'll likely stay miserable. Like my mother. I wanted to take the world head on like Janine; I didn't want to settle for what I felt was less than I deserved the way my mother perceived she had.

Janine and I were an odd pair. She was five feet one and at least 140 pounds; I was a foot shorter and weighed less than sixty pounds. With Janine by my side, the drunks and junkies we occasionally ran into seemed less threatening. Downtown Columbia was populated with homeless, panhandlers, drug dealers, and an assortment of other street denizens. We saw them all and could smell quite a few who loitered by the bus depot.

Janine always said she worried about me because I didn't have street sense. She had a point. One day when she wasn't with me, I took the bus to the Columbia public library. I was sitting at a table reading when a teenage boy asked me to go to the stacks so he could show me something. I assumed he meant a book, so I naively followed. Instead of sharing the finer points of literature he exposed himself. I wasn't frightened as much as I was offended. I ran to the librarian to report him, but he was long gone by the time she went to look for him.

Wherever we were—whether on the bus and walking around—Janine would say irreverent things about people, herself included. She'd point and say, "That woman has a fat ass" in one breath, then in the next add: "My fat ass is bigger than your fat ass," when the person walked away. She loved to make fun of herself and kept me laughing with the rude but funny comments she made about herself and everyone else. She taught me to embrace what made me different. Her self-deprecating humor might have been a defense mechanism, but it also showed that she accepted and liked who she was at that moment. Fat ass and all.

She spent a lot of time and effort educating me on black culture. Well, her perspective of black culture. She'd tell me black jokes, then have to explain most of the punchlines. She tutored me on body language and facial expressions. (*When a black woman looks at you like this*—she'd put her hands on her hips and tilt her head—*that means:* OH, NO, YOU DIDN'T.) She taught me the lingo, and she also taught me how to dance like a black person. Or more accurately, she tried to.

She'd shake her head in wonder while we waited for the bus. "White people just can't move!"

"I'm not really white," I'd point out.

"Close enough because you sure as hell ain't black moving like that. Now watch. Swish your ass this way."

She'd be moving in perfect rhythm to music in her head. I'd try to imitate the moves, but where she was all fluid curves I was more herky-jerky, but I was enthusiastic. I was a quicker study when it came to talking the talk. The first expression I picked up from her was, "Say whaaat, now?" in a lazy Southern drawl.

One time I tried that out on my father, right in the middle of our Taiwanese conversation. He stared at me, unable to compute what I'd said. So I repeated it even more slowly.

He shook his head as if to rid his memory of the sound. "No, no. You say *pardon me* or *please repeat that*." He clearly thought that manner of speech was unacceptable, even if English was his second language.

My parents knew nothing about my best friend, and Janine never came to my home. I guess I didn't want my two worlds colliding. My parents wouldn't understand Janine, figuratively or literally. While my mother didn't speak English, my father did, and he was naturally chatty with strangers, curious to learn about them. I didn't want him finding out about my bus travels because he would have made me stop.

But Janine talked openly about me to her parents and sister. One day she took me to her grandfather's house. He was a hotel bellman. The thing I remember most was his gigantic record collection of Motown and other black singers and musicians. Janine offered me an armful of albums, but I took only one. Again, my parents would wonder where I was getting albums from, so it was better not to draw attention to this other part of my life.

We were the oddest, most unlikely pair, but I loved her. Riding with Janine was the best part of any day.

In the spring we got a new babysitter who lived closer to Kilbourne Court. The Whitnecks were an elderly couple who insisted we call them Grandma and Grampy. He was a mailman, and they lived in a trailer three blocks away from our apartment. Their granddaughter, who was in the same grade as me, lived with them because her mother had disappeared. The old postman and his wife adored my baby sister and little brother and were very kind to all of us.

My morning routine remained the same. I took the school bus because I wanted to keep up appearances for the babysitters. The odds of them 1) noticing I took the city bus and 2) mentioning it to my parents was minuscule, but I still didn't want to take the chance; too many people would have noticed me walking the opposite direction. Plus. the Whitnecks were only one block away from the school bus stop, so it was convenient.

Afternoons were another world. School was dismissed at

3:15, but I didn't have to be home until around 6:30 to get there before my mother returned. That gave me three hours to explore, either with or without Janine. I explored every city bus route and would end up knowing them by heart. Each ride was its own little adventure of people watching, starting inside the bus station. I apparently inherited that gene from my father: I was fascinated by other people, except in my case I was more interested in observing them than talking to them.

Outside the depot young adults with backpacks, homeless men and women, and various shady characters loitered, casually asking passersby for money. Some of the panhandlers looked suspiciously well-dressed and groomed. Inside the depot there were rows of coin-operated lockers available for temporary rent. They made our school lockers look pristine, and I couldn't imagine why anyone would put their belongings in one. Some of the lockers seemed to never be opened, and I wondered if the person had forgotten about whatever was inside or if something had happened that prevented them from coming to get their stuff back.

I knew what my mostly insular life was like, so I wanted to see what everybody else was doing. The bus route from Old Columbia High took me to the Five Points shopping area on Devine Street, which was like Columbia's watered-down version of Manhattan's Fifth Avenue. The department stores there opened my eyes. I first noticed that people judge others by the way they look—their clothes, their shoes, their hair— once I started school. I was lucky in that my grandmother sent me nice clothes from Taiwan. And even if they were average clothes back there, here they looked exotic and unusually stylish, especially for a first grader.

I appreciated the clothes but often wished I could dress like the other kids in my class, but I didn't have the money for new outfits, and my parents would have viewed such expenditures as frivolous. But looking at pretty clothes was free, so I browsed the department stores, staring wistfully at the mannequin displays. I loved the smell of new clothes at Belk's, which all looked crisply ironed and fresh from the factory. After Belk's I would go to Dodd's, a five-and-ten, to look at knickknacks and stroll around. Next on the circuit were two smaller clothing stores, Tapp's and Berry's on Main.

I was morbidly fascinated with the three-story Dunbar Funeral Home on Devine Street. I found it ghostly—literally. I imagined the spirits of all the dead who had passed through its doors congregating inside the huge building and would hurry past the funeral home. A happier stop was the Pecknel Music Company, where I admired the musical instruments and browsed through the supplies and books.

Through both sixth and seventh grades, I rode the bus and roamed the streets of Columbia, both alone and with Janine. My parents never found out what I was doing. I had always been the responsible, dutiful daughter. And even though my father's sisters were exhibits A and B that Taiwanese girls could go against the family grain, it simply never occurred to them that their good little Taiwanese child would be somewhere other than where they expected her to be. And they were right; she wouldn't. But their very American daughter would and did. And in those two years I gained the self-confidence that would enable me to make decisions a few years down the road that would change the course of my life for the better, even as it profoundly disappointed my parents.

Chapter 9

發現

The older I got, the more I noticed the racial divide in Columbia. Maybe becoming friends with Janine made me more aware, maybe it was just getting older and more observant, or maybe it was riding the bus and seeing that the poorest neighborhoods seemed to be predominantly black. And it seemed everywhere you looked people proudly displayed Confederate flags and other relics of South Carolina's pre-Civil War past.

The United States is hardly unique in struggling with racial and ethnic divisions. It seems almost every country has inherent prejudices and biases between groups of people whether it's based on religion, ethnic heritage, or skin color. Even within the same group there can be divisions, such as the tensions between Sunni and Shi'a Muslims. The Hutus and Tutsis of Rwanda. The Serbians and Bosnians in the former Yugoslavia. And of course the North and South in the American Civil War. In the case of my ancestors, within the *yellow-skinned hierarchy*, Taiwanese are prejudiced against other Asian cultures including the Vietnamese, Laotians, and Cambodians who they consider on the low end of society. The Vietnamese call the Laotians uncivilized. The Japanese consider themselves the highest followed closely by the Koreans. It's like a ladder, with each culture assigned a rung.

Once when I was in second or third grade, my father invited a graduate student over to our apartment. The man's family was back in Kenya, and at one point their conversation turned to Southern blacks. I remember the man getting very adamant. "Oh, no, no, those black people, they're not like Kenyans. We are hardworking; they are lazy. We never take government handouts."

Even at my age I could pick up on his disdain. It boiled down to he was a "real" African, and Southern blacks were de-scended from slaves. So here was a black man who looked down on black people whose ancestors had been kidnapped and sold into slavery. Like that had been a choice?

Prejudices cut across national boundaries and can be passed down through generations. When I was little, from what I know, my family felt everything was fine when we were in Texas. After we moved to Columbia, there were a lot more Mandarin-speaking Chinese than in Rock Hill. Those who came over from the mainland in 1949 with Chiang Kai-shek looked down on the Taiwanese, and they passed that prejudice down to their children, who in turn passed it down to *their* children. Now remember, this is the perspective of my parents and their parents. Taiwanese perceived that the Mandarin speakers felt superior, like: *First you weren't strong enough to fight for yourself, and the Japanese conquered you. Now we're able to take over this island. You're weak with no honor.*

So when my parents—mostly my father—encountered Mandarin speakers on campus, he didn't want to associate with them. Back in Taiwan it was taboo even to marry a Mandarin speaker—as my father's sister discovered. The family shunned her for several years until he proved himself to be a hard worker, became a good provider, and they had kids. My grandparents finally grudgingly accepted him, but that they still never approved of the marriage shows just how deeply ingrained their disapproval was. The message was clear: we don't associate with Mandarin speakers.

The other thing that I noticed as a kid was that the Taiwanese looked down on the island's indigenous people, the dark-skinned aborigines who are culturally, genetically, and linguistically closely related to the ethnic groups of Maritime Southeast Asia and Oceania. So they look more Polynesian than Asian. Most Taiwanese consider the aborigines a lower class and call them mountain people, which is not a compliment. It's a slur intimating they are uneducated and underachievers. Not surprisingly, the aborigines have not assimilated very much into the general population, so there is a lot of segregation. Human beings as a species seem hardwired to be clannish. And worldwide indigenous people tend to be on the low end of the society totem pole. It also seems that in most societies those with lighter skin looked down on those with darker skin. This is the hardcore truth of what I've seen of stark, very clear-cut prejudice.

And it never seems to change. One of my husband's colleagues is a Korean-American surgeon who is married to a native-born Korean woman. Their son is a medical student here in Dallas. My husband and I were talking to the surgeon and his wife, who were beside themselves because their son had a crush on a Vietnamese medical student. Mind you, we hardly knew these people and his parents were not holding back. *We have got to get him out of that situation. He cannot see that girl. He is not going to marry a Vietnamese. We are Korean.*

The kicker is both their son and the girl he likes were born here in the United States. So they are both American by birth. But not in the parents' eyes. Of course, if he'd been seeing a white girl, they'd be thrilled. It was so uncomfortable to see that kind of prejudice alive and well in 2017. My parents—make that, my mother—tried to dictate my life too when I was in college, and all it did was make me assert my independence even more.

The only thing my mother would have hated more than me marrying a Vietnamese would be me marrying a black man. That would have put her into an early grave. I suspect it was a blood line purity thing. My father had friendships with African-Americans and welcomes most people—except Mandarin speakers—into our home for conversation and socializing. But they didn't want their children marrying another race.

I've never understood why the Vietnamese have such a bad rep among Asians. After the Vietnam War ended, many who sought refuge in the United States settled in the South including North and South Carolina. As a whole, Vietnamese immigrants were high achievers and many, many went on to become technology entrepreneurs and small business owners. Maybe because they have a blue-collar mentality whereas people like my mother feel more aristocratic.

Which leads me to another point: I don't believe my mother was racist. Skin color or ethnicity had nothing to do with her attitude. She thought she was better than pretty much everyone. She always had a sense of entitlement, which exacerbated her resentment at not living in the style she believed she deserved. I think not achieving what she wanted to achieve then made her feel like she had to prove herself to everybody near her.

Of course, my parents had no idea just how much my world view was expanding in those middle school years. Although my dad surely wondered what had happened to my vocabulary and syntax, which—thanks to my best friend, a soul sister who found it hilarious teaching me street vernacular—had taken a decided turn to the unintelligible.

One night he asked me to read over some letter he had written. "Is everything on this page correct?"

"Uh-huh, sho is," I drawled.

He looked at me with a pained expression. "Is that even English you're speaking?"

"Uh-huh."

"Sounds very low-life, uncivilized," he said, clearly frustrated.

Another one of my favorite phrases was, "Aaaw, maaaan..."

My mother would ask sharply in Taiwanese, "Where are you learning that vocabulary?"

"Kids at school."

Grammar aside, they thought it was rude, and you could see their irritation spike when I said things like, "Ain't nobody gonna be messin' with me," with a wag of my index finger, the other hand on my hip—very Janine-esque.

To be honest, I enjoyed bugging my parents. Unfortunately it was mostly lost on my mother whose command of grammatically correct English was still rudimentary at best; it was no fun teasing her with black slang if she didn't know what I was supposed to be saying in the first place.

I also experimented with writing using the jargon Janine was tutoring me in. "What language is this?" my father demanded. "Where are your prepositions? Your words are missing letters."

I was aware that the street lingo was like a verbal secret handshake. It identified who the home boys and girls were. It reflected a bond forged in financial struggle and being relegated to the have-nots. It was a statement about belonging and kindred spirits. My father's black grad student friend, Nathaniel, may have spoken the lingo when he was younger, but by the time I met him, he was immersed in higher education, so his world was academia, which has its own language. He also lived in a white neighborhood outside the city in suburbia. While he and Janine shared the same skin color, they lived worlds apart. I grew up concluding the greatest divide might not be race or ethnicity, but the size of one's bank account followed closely by education, although the latter usually determines the former.

I often wonder how different my cultural experiences would have been had we settled in Los Angeles, Chicago, Denver, or New York. Would it have been even more adventurous or would the size of those cities actually keep you more isolated?

⁂

The one thing I felt I missed out on the most growing up was celebrating holidays, especially Halloween. In both sixth and seventh grade, Halloween was anticipated by my classmates as much as Christmas. They couldn't wait to dress up in costume and run from door to door collecting candy and trying to scare each other. What did I do on Halloween? Sat in the dark mostly. My family turned off all the lights and stayed in their bedrooms behind closed doors to make our unit seem deserted and discourage trick-or-treaters from knocking.

My parents didn't celebrate Thanksgiving or Christmas, either. It was like the rest of the world was inside this festive snow globe, and I was on the outside staring in. Since I never got to truly experience these iconic cultural holidays, I tried to ignore them so I wouldn't feel as much disappointment. Most adults have great memories of magical moments or fun times with friends and family that they relive with each holiday, so to this day I simply don't have the same excitement I see in others about holidays, which in itself gives me a pang because I know I missed out on something special.

That said, once I had my own family and my boys were older, I made an effort to at least acknowledge the holidays. For Thanksgiving I'd fly my parents up from Houston and invite my husband's parents over so the in-laws could get together at least once a year. We'd socialize at my in-laws' house for a while then we'd go out and have Thanksgiving dinner— at a Chinese restaurant.

Still blending cultures after all these years.

Because of my friendship with Janine I probably spent more time with black kids than I did with the white kids at school or in our apartment complex. But my racial status was sometimes confusing. Our sixth-grade science teacher was a black man with a prominent Afro. One day he had to do a special census type of roll call. Basically, he had to sort his students by color, jot down the numbers and turn the results into the office.

This was not rocket science; for me it was more like Schrödinger's cat.

"All the white kids stand up," he ordered.

About one-third of the class stood up. Our teacher counted and wrote the number on his clipboard.

"Okay, sit down. Now all the black kids stand up."

The rest of the class got up, including the mixed-race kids who could have passed for white with their tan skin and medium-brown, wavy hair. The teacher jotted down that tally.

Since I was neither black nor white, I just stayed in my seat.

He stared at his clipboard, then took off his reading glasses and looked at the class. "There are twenty-five kids in this class, but I only counted twenty-four, so somebody's not standing up."

The black girl next to me leaned over. "Now, don't you stand up on the white side," she whispered. "You stand up on the black side. You're one of us."

The teacher repeated the roll call. The girl nudged me. "I'm telling you, stand up when they call the blacks."

I again stayed seated and again his numbers didn't match.

"This is very important," he practically begged. "Everyone has to stand."

So the third time he took the racial roll call, I stood with the black kids. When he saw me, his shoulders sagged. He silently shook his head, clearly understanding my dilemma, and his expression was apologetic. I'm not sure if he actually left me in with the black kids or perhaps wrote in an *other* category option. But he quickly finished his notes and resumed our lesson on solar and lunar eclipses looking visibly relieved.

✿

One day after school little groups of seventh graders were just hanging around. I stayed for a while, looking for something to do. My group was a mix of white and black girls. We split into teams for a war of words, which was basically a cuss-off. To me swearing was a display of solidarity, not really an insult. And it was almost always used with good humor among my peers, not as vitriol. The war of words was one of my favorite games because between Janine and my classmates coaching me, I thought I had mastered the art of swearing. But clearly I hadn't.

I stepped out into the middle of the "fighting" area. It must have looked very David and Goliath: a four-foot Chinese girl showing off my swagger and tough demeanor matched up against a normal sized seventh grader who was almost a foot and a half taller. My classmates were genuinely rough and tough; I aspired to be.

One of the girls on my side prompted, "Go, girl! It's your turn." She gave me an encouraging little tap on my backside.

I strode up to the opposing side, planning my verbal attack. If you want to throw down the gauntlet, go after the mother.

I stopped, put my hands on my hips, tilted my head and shouted, "Yo Momma's a horse!"

I pranced back to my side, pleased at the power of my assault, not immediately noticing the confused expressions of the kids on the other team.

"My Momma's a what?" one of them called out.

"Your. Momma. Is. A. *Horse!*" I yelled, with more emphasis.

There was a moment of silence, then the kids from my side and the other side howled in laughter.

My swagger sagged. *Oh, no, what'd I do wrong?* I was just repeating what I'd heard other kids saying. Perhaps *interpreted* what I thought they were saying is more accurate. More than once I looked up their favorite put-down word in the unabridged dictionary, which has quite the collection of profanity. I was pretty shocked to discover what cocksucker meant. But I felt no need to look up horse. To me the insult meant your mamma was ugly, i.e. had a horse face. I never understood how that became an insult because horses were really pretty animals. But I digress.

Several kids from my side pulled me back in and teased me. "Why'd you call their mamma a horse?"

"That's what y'all taught me!" I protested.

I patiently waited for more laughter to die down. "No. It's ho-ah. W-h-o-r-e. You know what that is, don't you?"

Actually I didn't, until I got home that night and looked it up in the dictionary. I think I'd prefer my mother to be a horse.

※

Wherever we were living, however crowded we were, my father would always have people over for dinner. Our little one-bedroom apartments were not amenable to such visits, but he invited them anyway. Most of our guests were graduate students in a variety of fields. Some of these students had families back home, far away in Africa or Asia, and maybe they were lonely.

People were drawn to my father because he conveyed genuine warmth and quickly formed bonds with new friends. By seventh grade I realized he was just importing some of his culture to the United States. His home village in Taiwan had an open-door policy, but my mother didn't grow up that way, and she would silently fume. Unlike my father, she was not gregarious and did not form attachments to people, which is why I don't remember her having any close female friends her age, not even among other Taiwanese. She needed a Janine of her own, maybe then she wouldn't have always been so resentful that my father was trying to fit in.

Sometimes after serving my father and his guest's dinner in tense silence, she'd drag me with her to a local diner rather than stay home and eat. But she'd be too angry to eat and just nibble at some of my French fries.

One repeat visitor was a fellow who went by John. He spoke Cantonese, so he and my father conversed in English. He came over pretty often, always unannounced, and they would sit in the living room, right beside the sleeping corner where our cots were, and have lengthy conversations that they both seemed to enjoy. I think John was my father's best friend, and I was happy for him. John made my father's world a brighter place like Janine made mine.

Another frequent visitor was a white graduate student, Roland. He'd come over three or four nights a week to go over math problems with my father. He was there so often my mother seemed to eventually accept him as part of the family and stopped fleeing to the diner when he showed up.

We were finally establishing roots, and Columbia felt like home as opposed to a pit stop. So of course, that's when we moved cross-country to another computer science PhD program, this one at Texas A&M in College Station. We would be gone before Christmas. So once again we started packing up, and in a flash it was time to start saying our good-byes to neighbors, teachers, and friends. The realization my bus-riding adventures were over left me empty, but the thought of leaving Janine left me bereft. I couldn't imagine anyone else ever making me laugh the way she did. Or ever sharing adventures the way Janine and I had. Even just someone to talk to on the phone. I don't even remember what we talked about. We probably just sat there making fun of people. She was the one person who I thought was hilarious. Maybe because she was the one person I could be my real self with.

My way of coping with our impending departure was to avoid thinking about it, pretending it wasn't really happening. That's why I kept our move a secret from Janine as long as possible. To tell her would make it real, and I wasn't sure how I would handle that.

I waited to tell her until my last day in Columbia. We were literally driving away the next morning. We both cried. Wept, really. It wasn't rational; it was primal. I think it was my first experience of genuine loss and grief. And for as hard as it would be for me, I think Janine suffered more because she was the one left behind. I would be distracted by having to adjust to new surroundings and getting to know a new city. In going through her daily life, I wouldn't be at the places she was used to seeing me, so there would be constant reminders of my absence.

Eventually we had to say good-bye and go home. We tried to stay in touch. I couldn't call her; long distance back then was far too expensive, so we wrote letters. In each one she told me how much she missed me. I dearly loved my friend Janine, but the letters started becoming less frequent, and I found other things to focus on. While nobody took her place as friend and co-conspirator, school and a new-found passion for cross-country running took up my time and focus. Had there been social media back then, it would have been easier to stay current with one another; instead, Columbia soon felt like a past life, and eventually I lost track of Janine completely.

It would be forty years before we'd reconnect.

Chapter 10

發現

$\mathcal{M}$y father assured us this was going to be a permanent move. I'd heard that before we moved to Alabama. Then we stayed eight weeks and bounced right back to South Carolina. I prayed that would be the case here so I could return to Columbia and Janine. But there was no going back this time. I didn't even have a yearbook to keep as a memento. The public-school system in Columbia could not afford middle school yearbooks.

The university provided us married-student housing, assigning our family of five to a one-bedroom, furnished apartment, and we settled into our new city. My new school was an educational culture shock because the curriculum was much more challenging, and I had to scramble to catch up, which I eventually did. Seventh and eighth grade passed and then high school loomed. Not much changed in our lives. My father continued on his PhD quest, my mother found more factory work, and I concentrated on schoolwork. My sister, who had been diagnosed with leukemia in late 1977, endured her treatments with little complaint.

Mingfang's cancer was a family secret. Their rationale was that if other Asians knew my sister had cancer, nobody would ever want to marry me because of my bad genes. I think the real reason is they thought it somehow reflected badly on them, on their own genes. Whatever their motive, my sister's illness was a dirty little family secret.

One of the biggest shocks of my high school years was my mother finally getting her driver's license. For years she hadn't cared. Then for even more years, she couldn't pass the tests. I cannot even estimate her number of failures. She memorized the shapes and colors of street signs. For the written test, she was allowed to use a dictionary. But she seemed incapable of parallel parking until she finally managed. We still only had one car but just having a driver's license was a big indicator my mother had finally accepted that we were not going back to Taiwan anytime soon.

When I was in eleventh grade, my father thought his dissertation was winding down and he'd be getting his PhD. So jumping the gun, he applied for a teaching position at Midwestern State University in Wichita Falls, Texas, and made us move there. But the job was contingent on his PhD. Once again my father did not get his PhD, and his contract was not renewed. So we went back to College Station, and I finished senior year at my old high school. By that time I had given up cross-country running and playing the cello; instead, I focused on preparing for college, even though I still looked like I be-longed in grade school. I had topped out around five feet and was still petite.

Our move from South Carolina to Texas marked the first time our family was not on welfare or food stamps. But not because we were doing so well. We weren't. My parents just didn't know how to apply for that assistance in Texas. Fortunately Medicaid followed us wherever we lived, so my sister had continuous medical care for her leukemia. My father had started another new PhD program, so he was a student again, with hardly any income. My mother's new job, key-punching at minimum wage, barely paid expenses. So of course they decided it was the perfect time to buy a house.

In 1982 when we moved back to College Station, a real estate boom was in full swing. Through a Taiwanese connec-tion, my parents were able to get a mortgage for a house in a new subdivision with no down payment required. God only knows how. But their mortgage for the tiny garden home was less than the rent they'd been paying in Wichita Falls. It's hard to comprehend now, but back then you could buy a house for almost nothing.

I think their zeal to be homeowners was a matter of saving face. When we left for Wichita Falls, my parents had proudly told many people that my father was going to get his PhD soon. It would be embarrassing to admit he still didn't have his degree, which would be obvious if we went back to student housing. My parents bought the house as a symbol of success. And it was definitely a step up. There was a living room, a dining room, and a kitchen stocked with appliances. Down the hall were a bathroom and two bedrooms. The master bedroom had its own small bathroom. The rooms were small, but every-thing was brand new.

My parents seemed happy about their new status as home-owners, especially in the company of friends. My siblings were also excited; my brother because he got his own room and my sister because she was sharing a tiny bedroom with me. It took all the money they earned to keep afloat with the new house. So if I wanted to go to college, I needed to find the money elsewhere. My parents were in no position to help.

I applied for everything I could find: a Pell grant, state grant money, the Texas A&M low-income program and other low-income scholarships, the Brazos County A&M Club Leadership Scholarship, and scholarships for students with good grades. I was approved for everything. There was no way I was going away to college. My mother forbade it; it was Texas A&M or nothing. But the upside was tuition for Texas state schools back then was relatively inexpensive, so there was plenty of money left over for room and board after tuition and books were paid for. I asked permission to live in the dorm.

You can imagine how that went over. I acquiesced, lived at home, and saved all the money. I started college in the fall of 1983 when I was seventeen. It was a breath of fresh air for me, a misery for my mother. I hadn't felt so free since riding the bus with Janine, while my mother did her damnedest to keep me tied to the family fold. But I slowly exerted my independence. For example, I volunteered to be an usher for a performing arts group on campus instead of coming right home after class. Baby steps.

After my sophomore year I went to Houston for a six-week pre-med clerkship—my mother had no choice but to agree because it was school related. But the more obvious it became that I was moving toward having my own life and wouldn't be at her beck and call to be her personal accountant, secretary, and interpreter, the more she clung. When I told her I was getting married, her bitterness and sense of betrayal were palpable.

My future husband and I met in January 1986, when I was visiting a med school in San Antonio. I was a nineteen-year-old junior at A&M, and he was a medical student at the University of Texas Health Science Center School of Medicine. He asked me if I'd like to go to dinner. I said yes. That night he asked me to marry him, and I accepted. We set a date for six months later. I was accepted to UT's med school and moved to San Antonio after we got married.

I wouldn't say our wedding was a festive affair. Both of our parents were angry and resentful because neither of us had asked their permission. His parents were appalled their twenty-six-year-old son could propose to a young girl he'd just met. They were insulted that they didn't get to meet me until the day before the wedding. My parents thought I was far too young and couldn't understand why I'd be so disrespectful to them. But the truth was, I knew if I was going to succeed, I needed to cut the cord as soon as possible. My mother would never kick me out of the nest; she would clip my wings at every given opportunity.

We had a Christian ceremony and a somewhat traditional Chinese reception. I wore a lacy white gown for the ceremony and a red, Chinese-style dress with a high-neck collar for the reception. Red is the color for good fortune. I'm sure my parents and in-laws weren't feeling all that fortunate, but things would turn out just fine for Doc and me. But it would take years—and probably the birth of our children—for our parents' resentment and anger to simmer down.

On Christmas Day 1988 my father was in Taiwan checking on his relatives. My mother and siblings had remained behind. I had been married for a year and a half and was in my second year of medical school. As I mentioned, Christmas was no big production, so nobody had anything special planned. That morning a little after 10:30, I received a phone call from my now seventeen-year-old brother. Mingfang had died in her sleep. She was thirteen.

I immediately drove to College Station. When my father

returned from Taiwan, we all went to the funeral home to choose a casket. My father was distraught; my mother seemed numb. I made the funeral arrangements, notified relatives, and prepared the obituary for the newspaper. But I couldn't reveal that my little sister died of leukemia. My parents insisted the truth be buried with her. To me, not being truthful about her cancer dishonored her memory.

Even if I understood their decisions and attitudes were influenced by different cultural prejudices and norms, I didn't agree with them then, and I especially didn't agree with them after I started raising my own kids. I'm not saying I go around hugging my sons every five seconds, but I am certainly much more engaged in their lives than my parents were in mine. Neither of my kids could have gotten away with spending three hours a day roaming the streets on a city bus. Even if that experience was one of the best of my life and had a profoundly positive impact, it was also prompted because I was left to fend for myself. I wanted to be part of the process of my kids learning independence.

I also wanted to give my kids the opportunity to develop a belief system, if they wanted to. When my sister got sick and realized she was eventually going to die from her disease, I had a crisis of the spirit. If there was a God, I couldn't understand how they could allow this to happen. Perhaps if I had had a spiritual foundation, I could have sought comfort there; instead, I felt abandoned by the universe. And because it was a secret, I couldn't even talk about it with anyone, not even Janine, so it became a constant weight.

While I've never converted to any religion, I could appreciate why others would find value in it. And when my boys were younger, at a certain age I wanted them to have some kind of moral structure, so there was a period where we attended a Bible church. To this day my kids can quote pretty much anything from the Bible. Then for a while I joined a group of homeschooling parents. Even though I'm not a homeschooling advocate, I went along with it because they had a good structure for their children. I'm sure my zeal to have structure for myself and my kids comes from living such a peripatetic lifestyle as a child. Structure provides security and a foundation to be your best.

Later we started sending our kids to a Catholic school. First, because parochial schools provide an excellent education and second, they're very structured. Those nuns have the discipline down. I'm fairly sure half the nuns I met were former Marines. Just kidding, but seriously, if you don't know how to discipline your kids, send them to a Catholic school. They have it mastered.

One of my sons became religious and reads his Bible every morning. And of course he eventually asked why his father and I don't attend church. I was like, "Son, we all just do what we need to do."

One fascinating thing about families is that the dynamics never seem to change. I'm still the cruise director, the one my parents and brother expect to make things happen. My brother, who now lives in Boston with his very American girl-next-door wife and three kids, is an internist. When my father had a heart attack a few years back caused by clogged arteries—no doubt exacerbated by gorging himself every day at an all-you-can-eat Chinese buffet—he insisted I be the one to talk to the cardiologist. So there I was, once again the spokesperson, even though my brother is the internist, and I'm a psychiatrist. Fortunately, I keep up with internal medicine, but the point is we still have the same roles as when we were kids.

It's getting a bit more pronounced as my parents get older. For a while they were spreading their social wings. In their sixties, they started traveling with other Taiwanese, like part of a group tour that took annual trips. I know they went to Niagara Falls once and other places like that. Then one year they took a trip to Brazil. My mother was very excited when she told me. But instead of staying on with the group, after they arrived my mother and father decided to take off on their own to stay with some distant relative of my father.

You know my parents could never pass up free room and board.

And thank God for that because the rest of the group was in a tour bus accident. The bus rolled and went over a cliff, and everyone on board died. My parents were the only ones from that tour group to survive because they weren't on the bus that day. It deeply traumatized them both. They might have gone on one more tour, but then they said: *That's it,* and they stopped traveling. I think the only place they go now is when I fly them up to visit my family.

I very rarely see my brother. It's been a couple of years now. And even that time and before, I had to initiate the visit. To be honest I started asking myself: *Why am I the one begging to see him, begging to see them?* And after the last time I flew out to see him and his family, it pissed me off that the effort was so one-sided because he never reciprocated. So I stopped, and the result is I haven't talked to my brother in about a year and a half.

That is one thing that is very different from living in the United States and in Taiwan. Here, you can move thousands of miles away and remain in the country. Taiwan is a tenth the size of Montana, just a little bit bigger than Delaware and Maryland combined. You're never more than a few hours away by car or train from your relatives. Plus tradition there has generations living together under one roof. In the United States, it's okay to have your own space for both parent and adult child. I don't believe that Taiwanese families like each other better than families in the United States; I just think they are controlled more by tradition and cultural expectation. You maintain contact because you are expected to. Here, people have the distance and freedom to slip away. Sometimes intentionally, sometimes by circumstance. My brother eased out of my life by choice; I lost contact with Janine because of geography.

While I was writing my book *Grown-Up Child*, which details the pressures and responsibilities often laid on children by immigrant parents, I spent a lot of time revisiting my childhood. I became nostalgic thinking about my times with Janine; less so reminiscing about my parents. I was old enough to see them from a different perspective. I started comparing my view and my life at twenty-five, thirty-five, and forty-five to what my parents' had been. And each time I did, I'd think: *God, what a disaster!* In my mid-thirties I was a working psychiatrist with a comfortable home for my kids. My father was on his umpteenth attempt to defend a dissertation and living in subsidized apartments. When he was forty he was moving his family cross-country instead of being content with his master's and getting a teaching job at a community college or high school, which would have made us financially secure. My mother was a good worker but never got promoted because she wouldn't learn English. Their choices were beyond me. *Oh my God you moved three times in a year?* You often hear of parents making sacrifices for their kids; in our case my siblings and I sacrificed for my parents' foibles. And in the end, for nothing,

In the summer of 1983, he took a three-month programming job in San Jose, California, and while there found out about Kensington University in Santa Monica, an unaccredited college of the diploma-mill variety that the state of California would later shut down in 2003. My father did not attend classes there; neither did anyone else. Instead he submitted proof of the PhD coursework that he completed at

Texas A&M. Kensington approved the coursework, and then they evaluated his dissertation, sending it back and forth to him for revisions a few times. This continued for a year, and in return for a diploma of dubious merit, he paid Kensington's high fees. (A Florida state representative who had to remove her degree from her C.V. after Kensington was shut down says she paid $20,000 for her degree.) But when Kensington approved his dissertation, he finally had his PhD—sort of.

Ever since then, when people ask if he has a PhD, he says yes. He even puts the Dr. title in front of his name. People assume his degree is from Texas A&M because he says that he did his PhD work there, which is true. But he doesn't claim that he graduated from there because he never did.

That unaccredited degree didn't get him the university professorship he had longed for. Instead, in July 1990 he was hired as a professor of mathematics and computer science at Houston Community Southeast College, where he remains to this day. You don't need a PhD to teach at a community college.

Whether he was driven by ego or shame, his pursuit had a profound effect on my life. But then again, we're all the sum of our past experiences, so everything that happened made me the person I am today, and I wouldn't change it. But if there was one thing I could have changed, it would have been to keep in touch with Janine. She had come to mind so often while working on *Grown-Up Child*, I decided I needed to find her and see how her life had turned out and to tell her I was doing okay.

Chapter 11

發現

*Y*ou'd think tracking down someone in the age of social media would be a snap. But not everyone is a Facebook darling. Not everyone tells the world their hourly movements on Twitter. And with women, their last names often change. I jotted down what I knew about Janine that would help narrow down the search

I knew her father was a welder but didn't know his first name. It's funny; her dad was strictly blue collar but made a lot more money than my father the sometime college professor did. But the family didn't have that much more than we did to show for it because Janine's dad spent most of it, she said, on gambling—cards mostly—women other than her mother, and things like cologne. I remember finding that funny at the time because in my mind cologne was for women. (My father didn't even wear aftershave lotion.) When Janine and I became friends, her parents were still married, but they would eventually divorce.

I wondered if Janine ever wondered why I never invited

her over to my apartment. She was very open about her family; me, less so. She knew I had a brother, who at that time went by the nickname Chin-Chin. She knew my father was a student at the college. And she knew my mother worked, which is why I was hanging out on the bus. But I never really shared what they were like. Nor did I ever share my Taiwanese culture with her the way she shared her black culture with me. I think because I considered my family's background something not particularly relevant to my daily life. I wanted to be accepted and a part of the world I lived in every day.

I knew Janine had a grandpa, the one who gave me an album the day I went to his house. She had a brother named Scottie and a sister named Renee. Whenever I called Janine, it was usually Renee who picked up the phone. She was a teenager then, and I can imagine her sitting by the phone waiting for one of her friends to call, only to be annoyed by some pipsqueak calling her sister. That's probably why she always sounded kind of disinterested when I announced who it was. Janine's mom, though, was always very pleasant and would ask how I was doing. My response was limited to a shy, "Fine, Ma'am," but her voice was always welcoming. I never knew her first name though. She was just Janine's mom, Mrs. Henderson.

After searching for Janine on social media and getting nowhere, I turned to newspapers. I did searches for Janine and came up empty. I tried Henderson and Columbia with no usable results. Then I took a flyer and typed in *Renee Henderson* and was stunned by what I found. Several websites listed her police record including an arrest in 2014 for transiency and providing a false name. Her mug shot showed a soul spiraling downward. I also found her obituary from 2015.

The obituary said that in 1983 Renee had graduated cum laude, earning a bachelor of arts degree in English at Coker College in Hartsville, SC. While there she received a scholarship to study abroad during her junior year and being fluent in Spanish, selected Madrid, Spain. She also was a member of the cheerleading squad, yearbook committee, and Commissioner Service Organization among others. She then went on to earn a master's degree in divinity at Harvard. After completing her graduate program at Harvard, she went on to study at George Washington University and the University of Minnesota and made Minneapolis her home.

The obit didn't explain how Renee had gone from academic star to police blotter fodder—although I had a hunch she was either bipolar or schizophrenic—or why Renee had died at just fifty-four. To me that was very young, since she was only five years older than me. But what the obituary did provide was a list of surviving relatives including her mom, Scottie, and Janine, whose last name was now Brown.

Armed with this information, I did another Facebook search and was pretty confident I had located her. I sent a message and waited, excited at the prospect of reconnecting. After several days had passed, I sent another message, but still no reply. Of course I started getting paranoid, wondering if I had done something I'd forgotten about to piss her off. Undaunted, I looked in the Columbia area white pages and found her mother: Phyllis Henderson. The address wasn't the same part of town as when we were kids, but I knew it was her.

It was a Saturday evening in late September. I figured a woman in her seventies would probably be home. I took out my cell phone and dialed the number before even taking the time to consider what I was going to say. Her voice mail picked up—so much for homebound septuagenarians.

I said: "Miss Henderson, I don't know if you remember me. This is Chiufang. I was a very good friend of Janine's. I've been looking for her. If this is the right number, please let me know. If not, please let me know it's the wrong number."

I was surprised by how fast my heart was beating when I hung up. I guess stepping back in time was stirring a lot of dormant emotions. Then about twenty minutes later, my phone rang. It was Phyllis.

"Chiufang, of course I remember you. I've just called Janine, and she just started screaming on the phone in my ears." I'm not an overly emotional person, but that brought tears to my eyes because I could just picture Janine jumping up and down. "Let me give you her number."

After I wrote down Janine's number, I said, "Miss Henderson, I want to let you know I've been looking for Janine for like thirty years. The only way I found her was because I found Renee's obituary. I'm sorry to see that."

She sighed, "Well, at least something good came out of something bad."

"I also found other articles; I'm so sorry about the troubles she had."

She thanked me for my condolences. "I'll let Janine go into detail about that with you. It's a sad story."

As soon as I hung up I called Janine, and it was as if forty years immediately melted away, and we picked up where we left off. I chided her for not responding to my Facebook messages and friend request.

She laughed. "Girl, I don't even know what my account is. Somebody else set that up for me. I don't even know how to Google."

We caught up on the vital statistics of our lives: kids, marriages, divorce, career. It turned out she was engaged, and the wedding was the next weekend. We talked for a while about that then I expressed my condolences about Renee.

Janine started by saying, "You know, I didn't realize we're from different fathers."

I reminded her I had suggested that when we were kids.

Her skin was very light, and her features were different from Janine and Scottie.

"Yeah, you did, but I never knew that one until later. I guess I didn't notice a lot. When Renee was a teenager, she started spending a lot of time in her room with the door closed. We just assumed she was studying."

I explained to Janine that Renee was probably isolating herself, either because she had started feeling paranoid or having mood swings. Mental illness can take years to fully develop although in retrospect there are always early signs that something isn't right. The problem with teenagers is that they tend to be all over the place emotionally because of natural hormone fluctuations so it can be hard to tell what's normal development and what isn't. And in the case of schizophrenia, it does tend to strike young men much more so than young women. There are a lot of theories why that is, but nobody has identified a single specific reason.

Research has also found that the onset of schizophrenia occurs later in women, so they may be more capable of dealing with the symptoms of their condition since they and their brains are more mature. People can control symptoms through medication and by decreasing their stressors. For example, establishing a controlled, consistent routine helps. Not everyone decompensates to the point of thinking: *Oh my God, there's poison coming out of the hair spray can.* The voices can be nicer, and they can decrease in frequency; instead of once every day, maybe they come every other day. But the symptoms never completely go away. And if you get into a violent or angry environment or go off your meds—which many do because they hate the way the pills make them feel—it can trigger a bad episode. And that's what happened to Renee. For whatever reason she stopped taking her meds. She ended up homeless in Minnesota and chose not to go back home. They found her in some abandoned building, sick and malnourished. She was taken to the hospital but died a short time later. The authorities emailed a picture of Renee to Janine on the computer so she could identify the body. It was her sister although she looked like a skeleton she'd lost so much weight.

I listened as Janine talked about her sister and grieved. Our conversation then moved on to other, more positive topics, and we ended up talking for about forty-five minutes. We said good-bye with a promise to stay in touch. I mentally replayed the conversation several times and made a decision. I told Doc I had found my friend, and I wanted to be at her wedding. He was very supportive and said I should go.

I went online, spent $800 on a last-minute plane ticket, booked a hotel room then called Janine back the next morning.

"Janine, I just bought a plane ticket. I'm coming to your wedding next Saturday, so I best be invited."

She was momentarily speechless. "Of course you're invited, China doll."

I gave her the name of the hotel in downtown Columbia where I was going to stay and the arrival time of my flight. We made plans to meet at the hotel after she got off of work.

I left Dallas the following Friday, excited and a little nervous. My flight landed in Columbia on time, and I took a cab into town. I checked into the hotel then texted Janine to let her know I'd arrived and would see her in a couple of hours.

I went down to the lobby at seven and sat down to wait. As time passed, I had several Marriott staff ask if I needed anything. I explained I was waiting on a friend. At eight o'clock I called her. Her voice mail answered.

"Janine, it's about eight o'clock, and I'm here in the lobby of the Marriott downtown. Just let me know if you're stuck at work or something. If I'm not in the lobby when you get here, I'll be in my room, 324."

At 8:45 I went back upstairs. I wasn't angry, just perhaps a little concerned. I ordered room service, ate dinner, then went back downstairs and called her again. Then I sat down to wait some more. I realized I wasn't surprised she was so late. Part of me had expected this from her. Not because she didn't want to see me; I knew she did. But she had been a go-at-her-own-flow person since the day I met her.

She finally showed up around 11:00, very excited to see me. She didn't make any excuses nor did I ask for any. I let it go. We took some photos together and looked each other over, reconciling the child we had known with the adult in front of us. The restaurant was closing, but the lounge was still open, so we went and sat at the bar. She ordered a drink, I had water. And we talked.

By the end of seventh grade, the school somehow figured out she wasn't really living in the school district, so they transferred her to a different school for eighth grade, meaning she lost all the friends that she had made in middle school. And the following year, she had to attend a different high school than all her middle school friends. So high school was just something she endured. I could empathize.

After graduating she enrolled at a two-year technical school but didn't finish. She moved up to the Washington DC area where Renee was living at the time. She got a job and met her first husband. They married, had a son, and then he bailed, leaving her a single mom. She moved back to Columbia and supported herself and her son working various jobs. She said she was only a few hours away from some degree, but it was vague, and I didn't push it. I could sense it wasn't something she wanted to talk about. She was currently working for Aflac insurance and then said she had just gotten a second job.

"Girl, you remember how we used to see those bums on the bus around the bus stations? Well, you won't believe what

I'm doing now. I'm working at the bus station as a dispatcher. All these people will be coming up to me begging for a ride here, a ride there. It reminds me of our days on the bus."

We talked about our old adventures until her phone rang. The call didn't appear to be a happy one. I assumed it was her soon-to-be-husband wondering where she was.

I said, "Hey, Janine, if you need to go home to your fiancé, I understand."

She shook her head. "No, it wasn't him. He knows I'm here with you. That was his mother. She's upset about the table arrangement for the wedding tomorrow. I need to go and get that all settled."

We hugged good-bye a little after 12:30 a.m. I watched her exit the hotel then went upstairs. After laying out my clothes for the morning, I fell asleep within minutes of hitting the pillow.

The wedding was held at a gated community's activity center. It was away from the city and wasn't the easiest place to find, nestled between some woods and other developments. I'm talking boondocks. But I had given myself plenty of time and got there by five o'clock. The first person I sought out was Phyllis, who greeted me like a long-lost daughter. Even before I was introduced, I had picked her out as Janine's mom. I was surprised Phyllis knew so much about me—apparently Janine had talked about me quite a lot when we were kids.

Janine grabbed my arm and steered me toward another group of people. "China doll, come here with me. I want you to meet my son. Here, talk to him."

Her son looked to be in his mid-twenties and was a little quiet—he must have gotten that gene from his father. But we had an immediate rapport. Janine nudged me in the ribs. "Tell my son what I was like."

So I pulled out a copy of my book, *American Sweetheart,* where I recounted how I learned to dance. I said, "Okay, this was what your mother was like when I was with her," and read him some of the passages. He started cracking up when I read the *shake your ass, girl. No, move it* THIS *way* section.

"Yes, that's my mom, alright. That is definitely my mama."

Janine had told me her brother Scottie had joined the Air Force after high school military. She didn't tell me how different he looked. He recognized me and came over, and we talked for a little bit. But he seemed edgy and didn't hang around in the main part of the wedding long and seemed to avoid Janine.

I asked her if something was wrong with Scottie. She shrugged. "When my father was getting ill, I kept saying you got to go visit dad. He said he would but never did. It's like he doesn't want to be around the family."

Again, I could relate because I felt the same way about my own brother.

Then an older gentleman walked up and took my hands. "You must be Janine's friend."

"Yes, sir, I am."

Now, that was a pretty good bet considering I was the only non-black person there. Literally. There wasn't a white person or Hispanic or any other ethnicity in sight. Except for me.

"I'm Alfonso, Phyllis's brother."

I introduced myself then told him, "I used to go to your papa's house; that's where Janine showed me all your father's Motown records."

He smiled then adopted me. Alfonso started pointing out Janine's cousins, aunts, and uncles on his and Phyllis's side of the family, which was a lot of fun. She had a big family—well, bigger than mine—and there was no way I was going to re-member all their names. But it made me feel warmly welcomed and part of the occasion. He introduced me to several of the relatives, and I was given a crash course on Janine's maternal family history, which was a lot of fun.

Our conversations were cut short because the wedding was about to start, and everyone took their seats. After the cer-emony was a sedate reception that soon started winding down. I looked around, surprised.

I went up to Uncle Alfonso and joked, "Now, wait a minute; what's the deal here? I've come to a black wedding expecting some dancing. I thought I was going to get to show my moves."

He laughed and shrugged. "I guess this is all they had planned."

Janine's cousin Roderick and Uncle Alfonso escorted me to my car because there were no lights out by the woody area. They also insisted I caravan with them back to the main street. I hugged them both good-bye and got in my car. They mo-tioned for me to follow Alfonso then Roderick pulled behind me. Once we hit the main road, they went their ways and I went mine. I was back at the hotel by 8:30.

The wedding was in September 2016. Since then Uncle Alfonso and I have become friends. I sent him a copy of *American Sweetheart.* He called me when he finished it and said, "Now I understand how you and Janine became friends. That put everything in clarity."

I told him, "When you have your next family reunion, you better invite me because you bet I'll be there."

He promised he would.

I've talked to Janine a few times on the phone since her wedding, and she remains her funny, irreverent self. At times I also sense a melancholy, but she deflects it behind an upbeat persona. I don't push, but I let her know I'm always there to be a sounding board.

She tells me how proud she is that I followed my dream and became a doctor. And that I grew up to be someone who did not suffer fools and wasn't afraid to get out of my comfort zone, like auditioning for the Dallas Cowboy Cheerleaders.

We have lived very different lives, but those early bonds remain, reinforced by other life experiences. She's one person who understands what it's like to lose a sister to a disease with no cure and the void it leaves forever. She also understands the different pain of having a sibling drift away.

I have been very fortunate in life to achieve most of what I've set out to. And I have more goals waiting in the wings. I hope Janine is content with her life now but still has more dreams to follow. I want her to have whatever will make her happy and fulfilled. And I expect to be right there, cheering her along.

The morning after the wedding, Janine called me at 7:30 a.m.

"Aren't you supposed to be on your honeymoon?" I asked. "Is everything okay?"

She snorted, and I envisioned her swatting my comment away like a gnat. "Girl, let me tell you what. I don't mean this in a bad way, but you were always my China doll. When I first met you, I always wanted to protect you, and when I saw you again, you were still my China doll. Now, what's interesting is that Uncle Alfonso called me at the butt crack of dawn this morning and woke me up. He said: *You better take care of that girl. Take good care of her and make sure she gets to the*

airport. She's a special girl. So you're his China doll, too—but
I did have to remind him you were mine first.

"So now, what time is your plane leaving?"

My protector to the end.

About the Author

CHIUFANG HWANG, MD, is the author of *American Sweetheart* and *Grown-Up Child*. She received her doctor of medicine degree from the University of Texas Health Science Center School of Medicine in San Antonio, Texas, and completed her residency in psychiatry and a fellowship in child and adolescent psychiatry at the University of Texas Southwestern Medical School in Dallas, where she lives with her husband and two sons. Chiufang is working on her next book project about the political tumult in Taiwan that ultimately prompted her family and many others to flee their homeland for the United States.

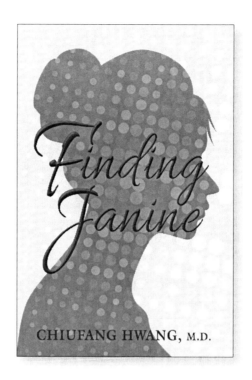

Finding Janine

Chiufang Hwang, M.D.
www.chiufang.com

Publisher: SDP Publishing

Also available in ebook format

Also by Chiufang Hwang, MD:
American Sweetheart: Still *Not Making the Team*
Grown-Up Child: *A Memoir*
Available at all major bookstores

SDP Publishing

www.SDPPublishing.com

Contact us at: info@SDPPublishing.com

CPSIA information can be obtained
at www.ICGtesting.com
Printed in the USA
FFOW02n0909090318
45511998-46252FF

9 780999 283929